Daniel F. Beatty

Beattys Tour in Europe

Daniel F. Beatty

Beattys Tour in Europe

ISBN/EAN: 9783337329013

Printed in Europe, USA, Canada, Australia, Japan

Cover: Foto ©Andreas Hilbeck / pixelio.de

More available books at **www.hansebooks.com**

"BEATTY'S TOUR IN EUROPE,"

IN

"FOREIGN LANDS,"

OR

"EUROPE AS I SAW IT,"

BY

DANIEL F. BEATTY.

DANIEL F. BEATTY, Publisher,
Corner Rail Road Avenue and Beatty Street,
Washington, New Jersey, United States of America.

1880.

THE FOLLOWING PAGES

Commemorative of my recent trip "In Foreign Lands,"

Are Respectfully Dedicated to

MY FRIENDS.

PREFACE.

IT has always been my desire to view the scenes celebrated for their antiquity and renown, to gaze upon the sepulchres of Kings, the crumbling ruins of ancient palaces, to breath, amid the towering summit of the Alps, the air where majestic sublimity reigns supreme ; or deep in subterranean caverns of the earth, look upon the sarcophagus of Prophets, Priests and Kings, and, approaching, read hieroglyphics that still withstand the shock of time.

All these mighty antiquities of ancient renown lay enshrined in traditions whose origin is lost in the dust of centuries. *To me*, the iron finger of time traces, amid the ashes and debris of ages, lessons written in an imperishable language :

> "Day unto day uttereth speech
> And night unto night showeth forth knowledge."

Lessons which all the nations of the earth can read, teaching mankind the immutability of our great Creator, and immortality of the soul.

> "For though Heaven and Earth pass away,
> The word of the Lord endureth forever."

To you, dear friends, I trust they may awaken the same emotions, and to whom I present these pages as a slight memento of my regard and esteem.

"BEATTY'S TOUR IN EUROPE,"

IN

"Foreign Lands,"

OR

"EUROPE AS I SAW IT,"

BY

DANIEL F. BEATTY.

THE eastern hills tinged with amber and gold, foretold the day would be bright and glorious. The waking birds sung out their sweetest carolings; the purling brook—"the incense breathing morn,"—all nature itself seemed to join in one general anthem of praise to God for the new born day—the one I had chosen for my long contemplated trip to Europe.

Friday, August 2d, 1878, will long be remembered and cherished as commemorative of the most eventful period of my life; not so much from the mere fact of my departure for Europe, as from the warm and hearty "send off" I experienced from the good citizens of Washington, New Jersey.

As the hour approached, the bustle and commotion seemed to intensify. Brilliant equipages, four in hand, drew up, one after another in front

BEATTY BUILDING.

of the BEATTY BUILDING, betokening, unbeknown to me, a preconcerted and well organized plan of action. Accompanied by my dear father and brother, my noble band of clerks, and a goodly representation of the citizens of Washington, New Jersey, I was soon whirled down to the depot—flags flying, children clapping their hands in childish glee, dogs barking—even the humble, dusty road-side flowers seemed to nod and join in the general acclamation of delight as we rolled by; but railroad time being no respecter of persons, the long drawn whistle and the rumbling of the approaching train abruptly brought our festival to a close, and amid the hearty congratulations of a score of voices, broken exclamations, and hurried adieus, the express train glided in among us, and ushered into one of Pullman's palace cars innundated with floral offerings and wreaths, and fairly walking on a bed of roses, I take the last long lingering look of the village spire, as it glitters and shimmers in the noontide sun—the gabled roofs of the distant town peeping here and there from out the rich green foliage—the crowd of smiling faces—shouts of merry laughter, greetings and huzzas, in the midst of which my little brother stands, crowding back the tears that spite of all will flow, as the thought of the tempestuous sea, dim forebodings of danger and the possibility of my never returning loom up in his young and imaginative mind—all these form a confused picture photographed upon my memory, which can never be forgotton. Like a pleasant dream, faces, voices, all fade away, as off we go, past field and meadow, to the great Metropolis—the modern Babylon of America—where we arrived at 4 P.M.

FIFTH AVENUE HOTEL, NEW YORK.

and were driven to one of the leading hotels, my thoughts busy with the pleasurable incidents of the day, which ever and anon were broken into by the arrival of fresh friends to greet me, offering their parting congratulations of a speedy voyage and safe passage across the briny deep.

Saturday, August 3d, was a busy day, what with looking after my financial affairs, the purchasing of Bills of Exchange from the leading Bankers of the city, the procuring of letters of credit, and the general detail of business inseparable from a contemplated trip across the ocean, filled every minute of my time, while the reception of numerous friends in the evening, rounded up another day of excitement.

The steamer on which I was to take my departure was to have sailed Thursday, August 1st, but having broken her shaft, she was delayed until Sunday.

Card after card introduced new friends and visitors, who, ushered into the spacious parlors of the hotel, indicated a warmth of hospitality which was truly gratifying to me in the extreme.

Night steals in—the last friend has departed, and I am left in solemn communion with my own thoughts; they wander back to the home of my childhood; again I see my friends of yore;—again I hear the dear familiar voices of long ago, and thoughts steal unbidden in my mind—what if I should never return—once on the deep blue rolling sea, with nothing but a few planks, as it were, nailed together, between my soul and eternity. Hidden and unseen dangers lay across my pathway, and as I peer into the shadowy land of the past, slumber gently shuts the door of fancy and bears me on its downy pinions to the land of sweet oblivion. Greatly refreshed I rose to greet the welcome Sabbath morn—sweet harbinger of rest—the best day to me of all the week—in whose sacred hours the mind can hold sweet communion with the giver of every good and perfect gift. The city bells ring out their joyous peals, but to me they sound not like those sweet Sabbath bells far beyond the hills—the bells that call the morning worhippers to prayer and song, ringing out upon the morning air, soft and clear, calling to each and all in a language of its own. But the hour approaches for my departure; all is again confusion, the carriage drives up to the door of the hotel and we find ourselves rattling down Broadway four in hand at a lively pace. Arriving at the pier we descry one of those leviathans of the deep, the city of ———, of the ———. As we roll down the wharf, the usual motley crowd greet our eyes, gathered together seemingly from all the quarters of the earth, crowding and jostling, jeering and chaffing among each other.

At length I found myself upon the deck of the steamer, surrounded by judges, reporters of the press, sailors and passengers, each intent upon the business of the hour, but all this babel and confusion was soon brought to a hasty termination, when the stentorian tones of the officer cried "all aboard."

Placed in a novel position and totally unused to nautical life, it may be reasonably concluded that I had many things to learn. The last premonitory admonitions were given—friends greeted friends for the last time—many weeping eyes, half choked sobs, exclamations of cheer, of courage and of sympathy, and we slowly backed from the crowded pier out into the stream, followed by the little tug boat my friends had chartered for the occasion to see us down the harbor and safely out to sea.

Boom! went our signal gun, the dying echoes reverberating along the Jersey shore, whose dim blue outlines stretched far away along the western sky.

The curling smoke from Fort Hamilton and the answering signal gun a moment after broke on our ears, as we glided stately down the bay, down towards the Narrows.

Thoughts of home, father, brothers, friends, all come trooping up into the memory, as if to take a last farewell; fainter and fainter the Jersey shore now recedes from our sight, and we pass the Narrows, we transfer our pilot to the little tug boat containing my brother and hosts of friends who had chartered it for the special occasion of seeing me down the Bay, and the reporters of the press jotting down the very latest items of interest, we part company, the heavy hawsers are swung off, and we slowly divide the distance between us, wider and wider, amid the waving of handkerchiefs, and the shouts of our companions and friends, which grows fainter and fainter as they drift astern of us, while I stand watching them long and steadfastly until in the distance it appears as a speck upon the waters far away, and now we stand boldly out to sea.

Onward we press, a wide expanse of waters before us, and land fast fading from our view. The bell announces our first meal on board the steamer, the sea is calm and serene as we glide through the deep blue waters.

Our eye scans the horizon and from all sides I see naught but the blue sky and the mighty expanse of waters, and the deep sea swell slowly and regularly rocks our steamer as its prow pierces the waves, shooting onward with the irresistable power of steam, and leaving behind a long narrow furrow of foam that marks our pathway. Occasionally a sea gull flaps its tired wings as though weary in finding a resting place, and is lost to view in the hazy distance. I descend to the saloon below, my appetite sharpened, and feeling invigorated by the fresh sea air, need I say that I done full justice to the occasion, unattended by the slightest disposition to sea sickness.

Sunday at sea—What a complete change from the preceding Sabbath; all is bustle and excitement, people hurrying to and fro intent upon their own enjoyment; no apparently religious veneration for God's holy day, but each left to the dictates of his conscience. At 9 P.M., a few well selected voices on the upper deck favor us with some choice selections, while the piano below resounds to the mirth and revelry of another happy party in the saloon below.

As for myself I stand alone, unobserved and yet observing, anon listening to the chorus of happy voices, and again peering out into the darkness that broods over the deep unfathomable waters before us, recognizing in its unpenetrable depths, the resemblance to that dark unfathomable Eternity towards which we are so silently yet surely approaching. Half-past ten arriving I retire to my berth.

Monday, August 5th.—I awoke at 6.30 quite sea sick, but with a full determination to overcome it if possible. I abstained from any breakfast, and proceeded on deck to the open air, conscious of an inward squirmishness that plainly indicated a rebellion was nigh. I returned to the rooms below, endeavored to eat, but could only manage part of an egg.

Repairing to the saloon I endeavored to divert my mind from my anticipated sea sickness—played on the piano and made the acquaintance of Dr. ——————————— 2 P.M. we descried a steamer bound for New York, north of us, and some 50 miles away. 7.45 P.M. saw a sailing vessel south of us, about a quarter of a mile away. Not a light could be seen on her, the moon shone down in silent grandeur upon the waves, reflected back in a thousand shimmering lights dancing in the moon beams, and stretching far away upon the dark blue waters of the rolling sea; one is involuntarily compelled to ask the Athiest—who says there is no God?

Tuesday, August 6th.—I changed my berth from the upper to the lower tier, as I could command a better view of old mother ocean. The weather continues warm, but I am assured that it will be cold enough in a few days, as we near the coast of Newfoundland.

In changing my berth I form new acquaintances in Rev. J. G.——————————New York, who occupies the lower birth right opposite, and Rev. J. A. ——————— New Jersey, the upper berth.

10.30 A.M. I saw a number of porpoises disporting in the sun, their round shining backs glittering every now and then as they came up to the surface and rolled playfully about. The weather continued fair, with a good flowing sea.

Wednesday, August 7th, we find ourselves considerably nearer the coast of Newfoundland, while the extreme cold brought overcoats in great demand. A heavy sea is running, and standing on deck I find myself wet through and through by a heavy sea. Very few are on deck, and nearly all sick. Clouds gather portentiously, indicating a coming storm.

We come suddenly to a stop—the ponderous machinery is motionless—an excited crowd gather around inquiring the reason why. Oh! only a screw loose, and in five minutes we are again on our way.

Thursday, August 8th.—The storm that I had predicted had passed over us during the night, and the morning sun peeping through one of the

OUR OCEAN STEAMER AT SEA.

port-holes of the steamer seemed to wink and blink at me with a sort of jovial smile, as much as to say, "good morning, Mr. Beatty, good morning."

Friday, August 9th.—As soon as the morning broke, and after performing my morning abulations, I betook myself to the deck to get the fresh air, and see how old mother ocean looked, arrayed in her vesture of deep blue. A clear but heavy sea. Concert to-night and I find my name announced on the bill to sing.

At 3 P.M. our attention was directed to the sporting of a huge whale in our wake. The sky, overclouded, gave every indication of rain, which at 6 P.M. was abundantly verified, making a wet night of it. The following morning, however, broke clear and beautiful. Nothing of any special interest occurred during the day worthy of special mention. The usual Saturday night concert, attended with speeches, jokes, and conundrums until the night was far spent.

Sunday, August 11th, was another fine day. The sun rose far away to the east, amid a molten sea of amber and gold, and the myriad waves tipped with their glittering sheen, sparkled and danced in their splendor, leaving a long train of light as far as the eye could reach. A strong north-west wind was blowing, and we were making most excellent time.

My soul, responsive to the silent prayer within me, praised God for such a bright and glorious Sabbath at sea.

How different this Sunday from the one preceding it, when all was revelry—now how changed, a reverential silence seemed to prevail and cast its hallowed influence upon all.

Several gentlemen insisted that I should aid in the devotional song to night, reinforced by a bevy of young ladies, who will not take no for answer.

I feel an inward satisfaction at an opportunity of being once again privileged to join my voice in the happy songs of Zion, and of praising God for His watchful care of me over land and sea. My room mate, Rev. Van Slyke of New York, favored us with a sermon, after which we dispersed to our several quarters with the usual good night salutations.

Monday, August 12th, we found the steamer rolling more than ever before, pitching up and down, tossed like a feather in the wind, amid mountain billows capped with white and glittering foam.

My soul was filled with deep humility as, impressed with the omnipotence and infinitude of a Great Creator, I gazed upon the solemn grandeur of the scene before me. Through wind and storm, sunshine and rain, wherever I might be, my soul felt exultant that I could recognize the power of the Lord God Omnipotent, and rejoiced that even terrible as His Majesty, I could still approach Him as my Father.

We were now fast nearing the Northern Coast of Ireland; in a few hours it was confidently anticipated land might be sighted. Glancing over my record I find that we had travelled 313 miles on our first day out, the same on the 2d day, 297 miles on the 3d day, 320 for the 4th, 328 on the 5th, 346 on the 6th, 341 on the 7th, and 334 on the 8th, up to 12 o'clock noon.

I had passed through varied vicissitudes, varieties of scenes on ship board, and had got quite used to my sea legs.

I had in this brief period passed through scenes varied and multiform in their character, some of them occupying but a few brief moments, yet how they live forever after, engraved indelibly upon the heart, which no touch of time can wholly eradicate, but are treasured in the halls of memory to be recalled only in after years.

At 8 P.M. the cheerful intelligence was announced that land was in sight, and a happier man could not be found on board than your humble servant. Never in the whole course of my life did I experience so much satisfaction at the prospect of once more placing my feet on *terra firma*, while a general clapping of hands, shouts of laughter and boisterous manifestations of general delight was equally participated in by one and all.

Tuesday, August 13, was the eventful day which commemorated my advent on to British soil. At 5.20 P.M. such of the passengers as had decided to put off at Queenstown had gathered their luggage, among which crowd I found myself, and was right glad to transfer my body corporal and worldly effects from the steamer to the little tug that lay steaming along side, which done away we went up the bay to the City of Queenstown.

The city, as I land, wears to me an ancient

aspect, and everything strikes me as so entirely different; the transition also, from "a life on the ocean wave" to that experienced on dry land, fills me with a singular sensation, difficult to express, but none the less apparent to me. Here I am a stranger in a strange land—while the very houses, railroad cars, quays—all strike me with an odd and peculiar look.

The city of Queenstown, built on the side of a hill, presents a commanding aspect, while the harbor is one of the finest in the United Kingdom; the entrance is well protected by forts on either side of the channel.

Among the passengers disembarking I noticed several Frenchmen, who were loaded down with trunks, bundles and no end of luggage. The eldest of the group, of fine commanding appearance, seemed annoyed at the number of packages, and proceeded summarily to dispose of a number of empty bandboxes by throwing them overboard.

At my elbow stood Pat with all his worldly possessions tied to a stick and slung over his shoulder. He stood watching them for some time and then broke out—

"Fhat a profligicy of them air furreners to be maken, when money's the poor old sowl would be glad o'the likes."

"Well why don't you ask him?" replied I; "there I added, see he is going to dispose of that empty old trunk in the same way. Go for him Pat," said I.

A merry twinkle played in Pat's eye and he gave me such a quizzical look as he retorted—

"Trunk is it,—bedad and fhat the divil would I be doin' wid a thrunk—and me go naked?"

From which I came to the conclusion that Pat's wardrobe was all on his back, and so enjoying his dry wit, I passed on.

Upon landing I found myself very hungry and

tired from loss of sleep, not having gone to bed all night, so anxious was I to set my foot on dry land.

It is now 6:15 A. M., which, compared to our New York time, would be equal to 1:45 A. M., which struck me as being so singular, that I could hardly realize it.

The first sight of a railroad car in Europe greets my eyes; built in a different style from those in America, they strike me as very odd and queer looking, appearing clumsy in their build, and do not possess the elegance of those of American manufacture.

After an half hour's ride of some 12 miles, I reached the city of Cork, and putting up at the

IMPERIAL HOTEL, CORK, IRELAND.

Imperial Hotel, I ate a hearty breakfast, and loosing no time proceeded at once to visit my first object of interest—Blarney Castle.

The ruins consist of a dungeon some 120 feet high, strong and impregnable. Descending to the basement from the outside we are led into a number of curious caves and natural excavations. At the north angle of the Castle, and some 20 feet below the summit, we find the celebrated Blarney stone, which is said to endow the person who kisses it with such persuasive powers, that no lady can resist his eloquence.

KISSING THE BLARNEY STONE.

There is a stone there, whoever kisses,
Oh! he never misses to grow eloquint,
'Tis he may clamber to a lady's chamber,
Or become a mimber of sweet Parliamint;
A clever spouter he'll shure turn out, or
An out-an-outer to be let alone,
Don't hope to hinder him, or to bewilder him
Shure he's a pilgrim from the Blarney Stone.

It is difficult to trace the source from whence

the stone derived its great reputation, but certain it is that the word "Blarney" is world-wide.

At this day it is more general to observe the custom without stooping to the stone, and our artist says:

HE'S GOIN' TO KISS THE RA'AL BLARNEY STOFE.

With quare sinsashuns and palpitashuns,
A kiss I'll venture here, mavrone,
'Tis swater Blarney, good Father Mahony,
Kissin' the girls than that dirty stone.

Bowing deferentially however to the mandates of custom, I kiss the stone, and proceed on my more interesting journey, by riding through the city of Cork on an Irish jaunting car. At 2:45 P. M., I left for the celebrated Lakes of Kilarney, at which I arrived about 6:30 P. M.

The Lakes of Kilarney are justly entitled the most beautiful in the United Kingdom.

Visiting Ross Castle and Island I took a small row boat and crossing the lower lake enjoyed its wild and romantic scenery. Large and magnificent mountains loomed up in portentious proportions in all their rugged grandeur. We pass the ruins of an ancient castle, built by some old Irish King, away back, I am told, in the fifth century. The scenery all along presents a charming aspect, far excelling in attractiveness our own famous and well known Delaware Water Gap. Here and there are to be seen the straw thatched roofs of the Irish peasantry, and occasionally one a little better than another, built in rough, rude masonry, at whose door the busy housewife, in true regal Irish costume, consisting of a night cap with immense frills, on her head, and her petticoats tucked up, was seen bent over the tub, with her arms up to her elbows in soap suds, scrubbing away for dear life, reminded me forcibly that I was in the Emerald Isle, and treading the sacred sod of ould Ireland, where St. Patrick is enshrined in the hearts of her peasantry. Gliding along the tranquil waters we enter Lough Leane or Lesser Lake, which is five miles long by three broad.

It contains some thirty islands, the principal of which are Ross, Rabbit and Innisfallen. Every variety of scenery can be found on this latter island—grassy slopes, beautiful lawns, and sequestered glades. It is not to be wondered at that it holds a charm to captivate the poet Moore, who has crystalized his beautiful thoughts into verse :

> Sweet Innisfallen, fare the well,
> May calm and sunshine long be thine ;
> How fair thou art let others tell,
> While but to feel how fair be mine.
>
> Sweet Innisfallen, long shall dwell
> In memory's dream that sunny smile,
> Which o'er thee on that evening fell
> When first I saw thy fairy isle.

I left Killarney, Wednesday, August 14th, at 9:20 A. M., for the famous city of Dublin. Nothing of real interest transpired along the trip, and indeed the transition so suddenly from the beautiful scenery around the Lakes, to the more sombre and common place scenery on the railroad from Killarney to Dublin, was not calculated to inspire me with any great degree of interest. Arriving in Dublin at 5:30 P. M., I proceeded, in company with Dr. Mitchell of Alabama, to take a ride through the city to North Wall Dock, a distance of about 2 miles from the railroad depot.

I visited the principal object of attraction, the Castle, the official residence of the Lord-Lieutenant since the reign of Elizabeth, its beautiful chapel built of Irish limestone and oak. On our way to the Castle we paid a visit to the Bank of Ireland, in College Green, formerly the Irish House of Parliament, and considered to be the finest building in Ireland.

Immediately opposite the Bank is located Trinity College, from which have emanated some of the greatest arts of our time. It covers an area of nearly 30 acres. The Cathedral of the Holy Trinity was the next point of attraction, erected in the 11th century. It is replete with historical interest, and it was here that the Liturgy was first read in Ireland in the English language.

The Four Courts was the next to demand our attention. It is a magnificent structure, and cost over a million of dollars. Over the entrance are 4 pictures worthy of notice : first, James the First abolishing the Brehon laws ; Henry II. granting a charter to the inhabitants ; John signing the Magna Charter and William the Conqueror establishing courts of justice. The Custom House and Nelson's Monument next command our attention, the former erected at a cost of two and a half million of dollars, and, externally considered, is said to be the finest building in the city. Left Dublin at 7:15 P. M. The boat made good time and arrived at Holyhead, Wales, at 1:15 A.M., crossing St. George's Channel. The distance from Kingstown, the harbor of Dublin, is sixty-six miles, and the channel is crossed in four hours and thirty minutes, average time.

Quitting Holyhead in the 2:10 train bound for London, my friend and guest, Dr. Mitchell, proceeded to ensconce himself in a novel position preparatory to his taking 40 winks—which just imagine, sleeping on a hat-rack, growling like a bear with a sore head, at my persistency in having the window open beside me, which let in a cool and refreshing draft, for the cars were very close and warm. As we dash through the country in the wee sma' hours of the morning I leave the Doctor to continue his disturbed nocturnal visions in the land of dreams, which no doubt were far from agreeable in his novel and uncomfortable position, while I, too absorbed with the constantly changing scenes before me, continued to jot down in brief the sensations I experienced, as we rattle through the land of the Welshman to the great city at the southern extremity of the continent—London. Now, gliding through beautiful farms, and anon passing, seemingly, stealthily by some old venerable ruins, whose ivy clad turrets looming up darkly against the moonlit sky bespeak the glory of departed days, around whose shadowy retreats and sequestered glades linger the hallowed story whose history has long since passed into the woof and web of romance; we slow up and pass over Telford's Tubular Suspension Bridge, situated about two miles from Bangor, and cross the channel that separates the island of Anglesea from the main land. This bridge is considered the greatest triumph of engineering skill in modern times. It took 1,800 men 4 years to build it, and cost $5,000,000.

The beach stretches itself far away in the moonlight, and reminds me of our own popular beach at Long Branch. Proceeding along the main line we arrive at Chester, one of the oldest cities, it is said, in the United Kingdom. It is beautifully situated on an elevated bank of the River Dee. The Castle is the principal object of attraction, erected in the time of William the Conqueror. We are now within six hour's ride of London as we leave this ancient city behind us.

Arrived in London at 10:15 A. M. The most wealthy city in the world, with a population of 4,000,000. Breakfasted at the Grand Midland, the largest hotel in the United Kingdom. I am informed that the furniture alone cost $425,000, but, for my part, I was not so highly impressed with its Table d'Hote, as I have been fully as well, if not better served, at the Fifth Avenue Hotel, New York,

Here I find myself—a mote in the sunbeam—amid millions of human beings where all the passions of the human heart run rampart, and whose lives full many are overshadowed by a sky of misery, the only stars which shine down upon them, are penury and want, and across whose dark horizon flits but few straggling clouds of happiness. One need to possess the graphic pen of its once most illustrious and distinguished citizen—Charles Dickens, to portray life as it is in this great throbbing heart of England.

MIDLAND GRAND HOTEL, LONDON.

Changing my English money into French, at one of the leading bankers, I left the City of London for Paris, via Dover, still accompanied by my friend Dr. M———, intending to make my tour of observation through London on my return. I took the short route, occupying only 9½ hours, while some of my comrades preferred a less expensive route, but which took them 22 hours.

Friday, August 16th, I found myself in the French metropolis.

I hastily repaired to my hotel and from here cabled to Washington, New Jeresy, the following dispatch in French, which was interpreted into English by my guide: "Beatty, Washington, New Jersey. Safe! Report, Grand Hotel, Paris."

This being in accordance with my promise to my friends at home, who naturally wished to know of my safe arrival. My stay in Ireland being of so short a duration that I was fearful I

GRAND HOTEL, PARIS.

would not get a reply in time without experiencing a delay I did not want to be subjected to. I was surprised that in less than four hours I received the following cable in reply: "Beatty, Grand Hotel, Paris. In line all," which private telegraph to the uninitiated meant a favorable report of my business and all well. The interpretation of these few words can be found out on referring to the key secretly preserved at my office, from where I always made it a rule to be daily telegraphed to as to the state of my business, wherever I may be travelling, either in America or abroad. I was glad to hear the cable indicated a prosperous state of affairs in my business.

Am I in Paris—the city of the world—home of the Kings and Emperors from the time of Julius Cæsar—the acknowledged head of European civilization—whose streets have witnessed the bloodiest carnage in the annals of history at one time, and at another resounded to the Pæans of Victory and Glory, canopied with arches of myrtle, the clanging of the hoofs of the war horse muffled as they sunk upon beds of flowers

THE CHAMPS ELYSEES, PARIS.

scattered on the pavements before them, while anthems resounded in praises to the King Maker —Napoleon—beneath whose imperial edict nations trembled and obeyed. How once my young and childish imagination went out and idolized this man when I read of his stupendous exploits of military daring and skill. How my heart rejects and loathes him now, as I reflect, look back and read the bloody pages of his history. One human being at whose command eternity seemed to have opened its jaws of death, and thousands upon thousands of souls were hurled into the maelstrom of destruction, sent unprepared before Jehovah's awful throne. All for what? France? No! for self—ambition. A throne, from which he, like Cæsar of old, could rule the world.

I made the Grand Hotel my head quarters, situated in the gayest part of Paris, adjoining the New Opera House, and in close proximity to all the leading theatres and principal railway stations.

This magnificent structure is entirely separate from all other buildings, covers an extent of 9,000 square yards, and its rooms are furnished in the most luxurious style. Its dining room is the most magnificent in the world. My first visit was to the Exposition Universal. It would be impossible to give any adequate conception of the Exposition, nor shall we attempt it; suffice to say, that it far exceeded my conceptions of all that is grand, wonderful and beautiful. Of course you are waiting no doubt with intense interest upon what I shall say upon the Piano and Organ question. Well—I must confess I feel somewhat embarrassed, one does not feel like bestowing eulogiums upon one's own self, perhaps it would come with better grace from my friend at my elbow, Dr. M—— of Alabama, whom I consider to be a pronounced critic. He says:

"The American Pianos and Organs beats them all, and Beatty's leads the van!"

I immediately proceed to search in my pockets for some slight token in honor of his golden opinion, but he laughingly retorts "that he is one of the Judges in the Exposition that cannot be bought," but nothing daunted, we proceed straightway to the place where the inner man is tenderly cared for and the cravings of appetite appeased, in honor of this flattering decision.

Having spent all day at the Exposition, we employed our evening by a visit to *he Mabille*, or Garden of Flowers. It is indeed a fairy scene of enchantment. Recesses, bowers and groves everywhere meet the eye, while the multitude of gas jets twinkle through the grass, or illuminate the Chinese lanterns festooned from the trees.

The next day, Saturday, with an excellent guide and a cab, was devoted to "doing" Paris in the most approved manner, the principal points of interest of which were:

The Madeline, Faubourgs Saint Honore, Palace de l'Elysee, the Palais Royal, the Louvre, Boulevards, Place Vendome, and a number of other important points which occupied our attention, until wearied with sight-seeing we repaired to our hotel to recuperate our energies, and cater to the whims and caprices of a sharpened appetite.

Sunday is a singular day in Paris, what with the teaching of Voltaire and the noted profligacy of the French people, the splendor of their churches and the magnificence of their cathedrals illy compare with that reverence for religion and the things pertaining thereto, that one is accustomed to in America.

Repairing to the Church of Notre Dame, situated in an elegant and gay quarter of the city, I found it mostly occupied by persons whose principal motive appeared to lay in the display of their attire.

It much resembles a Roman Temple, with its high altar supported by Corinthian columns composed of bronze bases and capitals. Many strangers visit this church for the purpose of listening to the singing, which is excellent, the organ being remarkably fine, some magnitude of which can be arrived at, when it is said that it contains 7,000 pipes. During my stay in the city one day I experienced a very novel sensation, that of ascending in a balloon half-a-mile above the city, from which Paris and all its environs can be seen at a bird's eye glance.

Need I say that I was honored by a Gold (?) Medal for the remarkable heroism displayed on the occasion. I slyly attribute it to the fact, however, that I was so high up that the expression of my countenance could not be detected, otherwise I am afraid I should have been accused of looking rather scared than heroic, as I was under the impression I should surely faint, and was heartily glad to reach *terra firma* again, not however, before assuring my auditors that it was a matter of every day concern with me, which I secretly believe was doubted by some, as I detected a few sly winks and nudges from the knowing ones, who apparently enjoyed my assumed *sang froid.*

Monday I continued my sight-seeing, and visited the battle field made so memorable by the siege of Paris during their war with the Prussians in 1871. Replete with historical reminiscences, well worthy the pen of the greatest French writer of the age, Victor Hugo, who has so skilfully surrounded the trophys of war with the laurels of peace, that one is at a loss to know where Fiction ends and Fact begins.

The night before the battle, that dread partition of time that separates the living of the morning from the dead of the morrow. The night before the battle, when in imagination one might well fancy we see Napoleon, standing with folded arms, solitary and alone upon the barren heath, between the camps of the two contending forces. Alone he stands, statute like and motionless—peering out into the darkness of the night, as if eager to consult the oracles of fate for the last time.

A yawning chasm opens up before him—no witch of Endor—but the Angel of Death appears before him, and bids him sign the blood-stained covenant with hell which shall dash unhappy France over the precipice, into the maelstrom of blood and destruction. It is done. The morning comes, the vision has vanished with the night, but on the blood-stained page of history, recorded for all time to come, we read the realization of the vision.

But France, proud unhappy France, still rises

Phœnix like up from the ashes of monarchy, to the freedom of a republic.

All is silent now—a solemn hush pervades the scene. How changed! The summer wind holds dalliance with the nodding daisys, swinging to and fro to the summer breeze, as if singing to the heart in a language unspeakable God's great anthem as sung long before by the Angel's at the coronation of the King of Kings at Bethlehem:—

> "Glory to God in the highest,
> And on earth *Peace*,
> Good will toward men."

The next day I proceeded to Versailles, the most interesting town in the environs of Paris, and 12 miles southwest of the metropolis. One can form a very inadequate conception of the magnificence of its grounds and palaces by a mere description. The home of Napoleon and the Palace of the Kings, before his advent to the throne. The grounds cover an extent of sixty miles, containing fountains that cost $2000 an hour to play, the most magnificent artificial landscape the ingenuity of man could desire, and palaces whose architectural grandeur exceeded in splendor any ancient or modern king, lest it be Solomon, and even of him it is written that in comparison with the lilies of the valley, even "Solomon in all his glory was not arrayed like one of these;" truly admonishing us that all the pomps, all the glory and magnificence of thrones, principalities and powers, shall crumble "like the baseless fabric of a vision," before the awful majesty and glory of

THE KING OF KINGS!

I left Paris Wednesday, Aug. 21st, by fast express train for Turin, Italy, via Paris, Lyons & Mediterranean R. R.

At Macon, situated on the river Saone, I stopped at the Hotel de l' Europe one half hour for dinner, and proceeded on our journey. Now we ascend the Alps, in fact I am told by a gentlemen residing at Florence, that even from Paris we commence the ascending grade during the first 100 miles on the road. I find myself agreeably entertained by Mr. Tilden, of Boston, Mass., a finer gentlemen than whom it has not been my good fortune to meet during my travels.

The engine puffs away lively as we ascend, now rounding this curve, now turning that, as zig zag we continue our course. It is 11 P. M., and the moonlight falls upon the Alps, bathing its snowy caps with amber light.

The scenery is grand beyond description, and never shall I forget the magnificence of the sight. The stars shine out in all their brightness, whose splendor seemed, under an Italian sky, undiminished by the brightness of the moon. I am filled with a solemn awe as I gaze mutely out upon the scene before me; and as I contemplate the glory and magnificence of God's handiwork, I am impressed more than ever before with the belief that all through my life God has ever been with me, to guide and protect my wandering footsteps.

About 4:30 A. M., we are instructed to change cars. I leave with some compunctions my fine palace car, and am transferred to quite an ordinary common Italian car. We are now on top of the Alps.

"To me they seemed the barriers of a world,
Saying thus far, and no farther!
* * * * * * * *
My wandering thoughts, my only company,
And they before me still, oft as I looked
A strange delight, mingled with fear, came o'er me,
A wonder as at things I had not heard of.
A something that informs him 'tis a moment
Whence he may date henceforward and forever."

Here is located the Italian Custom House, where I am obliged to show my passport and have my baggage overhauled. This being the first occasion of showing my passport, as at Queenstown and Paris my baggage was simply examined. At 5:30 A. M., we pass through Mount Cenis Tunnel. I had an excellent view of the entrance from the French side, as our train stopped some little time before entering. It occupied just 22 minutes to pass through the tunnel, and on emerging on the other side the scenery of the Alps was grand in the extreme.

Arrived at Turin, 9 A. M., where after breakfasting at the Grand Hotel de l' Europe, opposite

GRAND HOTEL DE L'EUROPE, TURIN.

the King's Palace, I set out via Alexandria, for Genoa, the birth place of Christopher Columbus.

A monument erected to his memory is situated near the railway station. At the foot of the statue a figure of America is kneeling, the whole being composed of white marble. After dining at the Hotel De Ville, I set out to visit the Cathedral of San Lorenzo. It was erected in the eleventh century, gothic in style, and built of white and black marble. It contains many interesting scriptural relics, among which I was shown the dish upon which our blessed Saviour is supposed to have ate the Last Supper.

So valuable was it considered that the Jews lent the Genoese 4,000,000 francs on it within fifty years.

The Church of L'Annunciata, second in size to the Cathedral, was next visited. It is truly a magnificent building, rich in decorations and highly colored frescoes. The rich marble in the interior gives it an appearance of great beauty. The Palazzo Doria situated in the centre of a beautiful garden which extends to the sea, forms a fine feature in the picturesque scenery of Genoa. In the garden are walks of cypress and orange; also fountains, statues and vases.

Engaging the service of a boatman, I enjoyed a ride upon the Gulf of Genoa, which opens out into the broad Mediterranean, obtaining a good view of the city, which rises to the height of 500 feet above the sea.

VIEW OF GENOA, ITALY.

I was not so favorably impressed with the city the next day, as I find the streets dirty in the extreme. At 1.10 P. M., I leave for Pisa. The train passes through a long tunnel on leaving the city, as Genoa is built upon an eminence overlooking the sea. For the first 100 miles we appear to be constantly diving in and out of tunnels. Now gliding along the borders of the beautiful Mediterranean Sea, and again plunging into the murky darkness of one of these subterranean caverns at the rate of 60 miles an hour.

All along the route the country presents a bleak barren prospect, reminding me of the illustrations I have often seen of the Holy Land. When about twenty miles or so from Pisa, the country looked less wild and gradually farms and farm houses gave tokens of thrift and industry.

I found Pisa an ancient and much decayed city, chiefly remarkable for its Cathedral, and Leaning Tower. The former is an interesting specimen of the style of architecture of the 11th century, built in the form of a Latin cross. Its 12 altars were designed by Michael Angelo. The leaning tower is 190 feet high, overhanging the base some 15 feet, and has occupied this leaning position for over six centuries. The ascent is made by 295 steps, the view from the top being extensive and beautiful.

PISA AND THE LEANING TOWER.

Sallying forth at 4. A. M., filled with an intense desire to reach the great city of Rome, I take the

4:53 A. M., train bound for the Immortal City. From Pisa to Rome the country is flat, and nothing of special interest to attract attention.

The railway enters the city by an opening made for its passage, near the Port Maggiorie, and has its terminus at the Piazza di Termini.

As I approached the city I could see the ancient ruins of the old wall, which seemed to remind me of Jerusalem and Palestine; an irregular zigzag structure, mainly of brick, with towers, bastions and all kinds and forms of masonry.

It would be difficult for me to describe my feelings; to think that I should all my life desire to see Rome, and now I can hardly realize that my eyes behold it. It is more like a vision than a reality.

> I am in Rome! oft as the morning ray
> Visit these eyes, waking, at once I cry,
> Whence this excess of joy? What has befallen me.
> And from within a thrilling voice replies:
> "Thou art in Rome the city that so long
> Reigned absolute; the mistress of the world."

On arriving at the hotel I experienced considerable inconvenience, as I found no one who could speak to me in English. You can therefore, perhaps imagine my discomforture, when, hungry and tired, I had ordered a fine rare steak, and after waiting in mute expectancy of shortly being able to appease the cravings of my appetite, the servant approached and deferentially proceeded to set before me a flagon of beer. To this I mildly demurred, and after considerable dumb pantomime which he neither would or could understand, I resorted to the landlord in despair, whom I found could speak a little broken English, and to whom I endeavored to make my wants and wishes known as best I could, and with tolerable success.

After being served with some sort of dish I certainly did not order, but which I found quite acceptable in the absence of anything else, I endeavored to make the most of it, after which I conveyed the information that I should like a cab, and equipped with a Guide book of Rome, I instructed the driver to take me to the great

VIEW OF ROME.

Cathedral St. Peters, which information I conveyed by pointing it out to that distinguished worthy on a map I had with me.

St. Peters at Rome, the home of the Popes, is the largest cathedral in the world, and cost $16,000,000. On entering this stupendous edifice one cannot fail to be impressed with the grandeur of the interior, with its statutes, vestibules, massive piers, arches, and dome, which have commanded the admiration of multitudes. The covering over the high altar alone cost $100,000.

A splendid view of the city is had on ascending the dome. Viewing persons passing along the pavement below, we can scarcely realize them to be human beings, so diminutive do they appear.

St. Maria Maggiore is the most beautiful church of its kind in existence. In a small chapel underneath the high altar are preserved the boards of the manger in which the Saviour was laid after his birth.

St. Clemente is remarkable for the subterranean basilica which has recently been excavated beneath it. They probably contain the earliest examples of christian paintings, and date from the 8th century.

I spent Sunday in the Holy City. It was a delightful Sabbath. The chiming of many bells proclaimed the hour of worship.

In the evening, under the custody of a reliable guide, I visited the Colosseum, the greatest of

THE COLOSSEUM.

antique structures, built in honor of Titus, and on which it is said 60,000 Jews were engaged ten years. It is said to have seated 87,000 people. To obtain entrance at night it is necessary to have a ticket from the Commandant de Place.

Looking back in after years, it seems to me, I can live over again my experiences and sensations during that eventful moonlight night, so well expressed by the poet Byron :

" I do remember me that in my youth,
When I was wandering, upon such a night,
I stood within the Colosseum's wall
Midst the chief relics of almighty Rome.
The trees which grew along the broken arches
Waved dark in the blue midnight, and the stars
Shone through the rents of ruin ; from afar
The watch-dog bay'd beyond the Tiber ; and
More near, from out the Cæsar's Palace came
The owl's long cry, and interruptedly,
Of distant sentinels the fitful song
Begun and died upon the gentle wind.
Some cypresses beyond the time-worn breach
Appeared to skirt the horizon ; yet they stood
Within a bow shot where the Cæsars dwelt,
And dwell the tuneless birds of night, amid
A grove, which springs through leveled battlements,
And twines its roots with the imperial hearths ;
Ivy usurps the laurels's place of growth ;
But the gladiator's bloody circus stands,
A noble wreck in ruinous perfection,
While Cæsar's chambers and the Augustan halls
Grovel on earth in indistinct decay."

In the vineyard northeast are the remains of the Baths of Titus, founded on a portion of the Golden House of Nero.

Truly are the predictions of our Saviour fulfilled, for shorn of all its glory, setting in the ashes of its gloom, and desolation, nothing remains but a heap of crumbling ruins.

At 9:20 A. M., I quitted Rome for Naples. The day is lovely, a gentle breeze stirs amid the foliage, with hardly a cloud floating in the clear blue Italian sky. The country from Rome to Naples bears a strong resemblance to the scenery surrounding the Holy Land. The mountains wear a barren look, and the very cattle, lean and poor, grazing on the hill side, seem to bear evidence of the sterility of its soil. The people bear a strong resemblance to the Arab, and the women are to be seen working in the field.

Very few travel first class through Italy, and I therefore find myself most of the time travelling alone. I arrive at Naples at 5:20 P. M. It is a favorite retreat of the wealthy Romans. The situation of Naples is as fine as can be imagined, being partly seated on a spacious bay, upon the shores of which are magnificent villas and gardens. There are some 300 churches in this city, many of them remarkable for their architectural beauty.

As I approached the city I obtained a view of Mount Vesuvius, over which a cloud hung, somewhat intercepting a full view of this, the most active volcano in the world.

At this season of the year and in this climate, one must go to bed well protected, otherwise it will be difficult to obtain any sleep, owing to the depredations of the bloodthirsty and insinuating mosquito, who present their bills for payment long in advance of the landlord, in fact so importunate were they in their demands, that I found it necessary to put an end to their further annoyance by leaving them in full possession of my chamber, to quarrel among themselves over their lost opportunity of a splendid banquet.

Desirous of visiting Mount Vesuvius, and to behold the rising of the sun at its summit, set out to procure me a conveyance.

The hour was extremely early, 1:50 A. M., but nothing daunted at the prospect of the drive before me, or the obscure and toilsome ascent up the mountains, I accosted a very forbidding-looking fellow, the driver of a cab, of whom there are any number to be found in the city of Naples ready to charge strangers any extortionate sum to convey them to the summit of the mountain. They dream away their time in their cabs wherever they may be located, while their horses seem to sleep in their harness, as, hitched to their cabs, they stand ready at a moment's notice to go any desired direction.

"Halloo! there"! cried I, as he lazily descended from his seat and viewed me from head to foot with his sinister eye, and taking off his cap to salute me, he answers:

"Si, Signore, Si."

"How much to the mountains and back," I inquired, returning his glances with some degree of mistrust.

"20 francs, Signore."

"Why man that's nearly twice as much as you ought to charge."

He shrugged his shoulders and made some remark in Italian which I could not understand, except "Diavilo," from which I inferred he was quietly consigning my soul to the lower regions for finding fault with his charges.

Knowing these people to be very vindictive, I made as though I would abandon my project.

"Ha, il mio cabretto a 15 franc," replies he.

"I'll give you 12 francs and that's all," I answered, unconcerned whether he accepted or rejected the offer.

His eyes seem to sparkle, for he caught sight of my diamond stud as it glittered in the rays of the light, but which I was not conscious of, only as I recalled the circumstance afterwards.

Conveying to me, in his broken English, the fact that he would accept the sum named, I was about to accept and enter the vehicle, when I was suddenly grasped by the arm, and a stranger accosted me.

Turning around I saw a gentleman, tall and of commanding address.

"Beg pardon," said he, "but where do you intend going at this extremely early hour?"

Glad that I had met some one who could speak English, I replied:

"To Mount Vesuvius."

"Well, I should like to see you for just a moment," and giving me a gentle pull by the sleeve, and a movement of the head, as though conveying the idea that he wanted to be out of ear shot of the driver.

As I turned an inquiring look upon the stranger, I mechanically obeyed, with considerable confidence, as I fairly worshipped any one who could speak my own native tongue. Stopping near a corner, some 50 yards away, he continued in a hasty undertone:

"Do you really intend to go to Mount Vesuvius at this hour of the morning?"

Assuring him that such was my intentions, he looked at me in a sort of astonished manner, which gave me to understand that something was wrong, the nature of which I could not divine.

"Well,"—he replied—"I suppose you are a stranger in these parts?"

Assuring him I was, he continued:

"My friend, it is none of my business, but I will give you a bit of advise. Don't you go—not a bit of it. If you attempt the trip at this early hour, you will in all probability be robbed and perhaps murdered. Why, the lustre of your diamond and watch chain, and the probability of your having a large sum of money about your person, will be the means of exposing you to their violence and perhaps murder."

"Murder!" gasped I.

"Why, of course, these men belong to the *lazzaroni*—see how angry and impatient he grows as he stands there expecting your return."

"I am ten thousand times obliged to you. I must acknowledge it was thoughtlessness on my part, and not aware of the"—

"Never mind," interrupted he, "we must be moving to avoid further trouble."

I hallooed back to him that I guessed I would not go—but wait till morning. Whether he understood my answer or not I could not say, but rushing up to us with oaths and threats of violence, he gave me to understand that I had forfeited my 12 francs.

Nothing daunted, my new-found friend motioned him away, upon which his anger became intense, and plunging his hand into his vest, I plainly discerned the gleam of a poignard, as he scowled at me with intense malignity.

At this movement my companion drew forth a revolver, and looking him straight in the eye with a determination which I knew meant business, he covered our retreat beyond the hearing of his rage and curses.

I offered to recompense my English friend in any way in my power, but he would not listen to anything of the kind. Assuring him that I should always bear him in grateful remembrance, we parted at the hotel, the recipient of my warmest wishes, which I felt to be totally inadequate to the services he had rendered me.

POMPEII AND MOUNT VESUVIUS.

At 7:30 I once more essayed to carry out my

original intentions, and had the good fortune to
fall in company with a gentleman contemplating
the same journey, who with the advice and as-
sistance of our hotel proprietor, secured for us a
first-class cenveyance and a reliable driver, and
again we were off for old hoary-headed Mount
Vesuvius ; by the way, the ruins of Pompeii,—
the most wonderful of the antiquities of Europe,
recalling the actual presence of a Roman town as
it existed 2,000 years ago.

I arrived at the ruins at 10:50, and employing
the services of a guide found myself in this de-
serted city traversing its carefully paved and
well worn streets. The houses generally extend
in unbroken lines, in an excellent state of preser-
vation and bearing the appearance of their being
actually inhabited. But their voiceless chambers are tenantless, and the people that once
thronged its streets and theatres are mingled
with the dust and debris of nearly 2,000 years
ago.

What a flood of thought comes pouring in
upon me as I gaze upon its walls, its gates, streets,
houses, temples, fountains and theatres. Turning to the right or to the left, as you wander from
street to street, you can almost fancy its inhabitants would momentarily come out to greet you.

The prophesy of Isaiah is forcibly presented to
my mind :

"The defenced city shall be desolate, and the
habitations forsaken, and left like a wilderness."
—ISAIAH, XXVII., 10.

" But the cormorant and the bittern shall possess it ; the owl also and the raven shall dwell in
it, and he shall stretch out upon it the line of
confusion and the stones of emptiness."—ISAIAH,
XXXIV., 11.

Empty and desolate indeed were its habitations, and the silence of centuries enshrouded the darkness of its sepulchres and tombs. Ascending the elevated pavement of the Forum its position commanded a magnificent view of Vesuvius and the Appenines, and I could look with awe and veneration upon the silent city, the home of Cicero, Homer and Ovid, whose history, wrapped in the obscurity of over a hundred centuries, still proclaim them to be the most distinguished poets of ancient, if not of modern times.

We will turn our attention now to Vesuvius, that rears her magnetic cone in the distance, the only volcanic mountain on the continent of Europe, and one of the most active in the world; from the earliest ages on record its eruptions have occurred at intervals of a few years. It rises in the midst of the plain of Campania, and is surrounded on the north and east by mountains of Appennine limestone. It is open to the plain of Naples on the west, and on the south its base is reached by the sea.

Ascending gradually we leave the cultivated fields and vineyards behind us, occasionally traversed by streams of old lava, black, rough and sterile, and finally reached the Hermitage, a convent where a few monks keep a sort of an inn for the visitors of Vesuvius. Farther up we traverse large fields of lava extremely rough. At the base of the cone we prepared for the ascent over a heap of crumbling ashes and cinders, extremely steep.

In another hour we found ourselves on extremely hot ground, intolerable to the hand and fatal to the soles of our shoes; it steamed with hot vapors and was covered with beautiful efforescences of sulphur. Smoke issued from numerous crevices, at the entrance of which a piece of paper or stick took fire.

Stooping low we could hear, as it were, a liquid boiling. The hard but thin crust upon which we stood had apparently settled down in some places.

A few steps more and we arrive at the very summit of the cone, and with bated breath we gaze into the crater, down its precipitous depths, 400 or 500 feet. When in action Vesusvius presents a magnificent spectacle.

Down to the reign of Titus Vespasian there is no evidence of any volcanic activity, but in the first year of his reign, A. D. 79, it burst forth with destructive fury, overwhelming the flourishing cities of Hurculaneum and Pompeii, all traces of which were lost for upwards of 1600 years, and were only accidentally discovered during the last century.

Another incident happened me on my descent of Mount Vesuvius, which impressed upon my mind vivid remembrances of the place, which I shall not in all probability ever forget.

ATTACKED BY ROBBERS.

I had wandered away from my companions and

guide in search of some mementoes to bring back with me on my return, and was intently examining a curious specimen of mineral which had encrusted itself in the scoria at my feet, when I was suddenly confronted by four as rough looking customers, as it was ever my ill fortune to see.

They evidently enjoyed my surprise on finding myself thus suddenly, as it were, in their power. I looked around for my companions and guide, but as I had descended a slight declivity in the mountains, they were hid from sight.

I had not, even after my experience of the morning, taken the precaution to arm myself, but fortunately had left my valuables at the hotel, with the exception of a small sum of money.

One of them approached me flourishing a bright stilletto in the air, while the others set up a low, brutal laugh.

Addressing me in Italian, the nature of which I could only surmise, I saw it would be worse than useless to make any defence, and knowing their intent I hastily besought them to release me and they were at liberty to take all I possessed, while I hurriedly put my wits to work as to how I should escape from their meshes, for I had, indeed, fallen in with another band of robbers, with which this mountain is infested.

I was not many moments in making up my mind, indeed, if I had been, in all probability I should never have had the opportunity of jotting down my travels in Foreign Lands.

Hastily drawing forth a huge business wallet, which I noted they viewed with grim satisfaction. I threw it with all my strength in the direction just opposite to the way I wished to escape.

Eager to be the first possessor of the treasure, they all made a rush for it, and during the confusion that ensued I bounded like a deer down the mountain side, running for dear life, while I heard the crack of their pistols, and the whiz of their bullets past my head. I was not long I assure you in regaining my companions, to whom I related my experience. Receiving a reprimand from my guide, I inwardly thanked providence that I had again made such a narrow escape.

THE CRATER OF VESUVIUS AS I SAW IT.

I was heartily glad to get back to Naples, and from thence I took my departure for Rome again. Seven long hours travelling through a hot Italian sun, brought me once more to the "Eternal City." Here in company with an old resident of Rome, whose acquaintance I had made on the train from Naples, I rode about the city and visited some of the principal objects of interest.

I was so well pleased with my experience that I concluded to spend another day. So the next morning I was provided with an excellent guide, costing me 24 francs, which I by no means regretted, and proceeded to visit the ancient ruins which Rome holds enshrined, of all the sublimest monuments of history and antiquity. Every spot is sacred to the memory of departed glories. Its ruins scattered in vast and shapeless masses over

INTERIOR OF THE COLOSSEUM.

the Seven Hills impress us with solemn awe, for they stand in lonely majesty, with groves of funereal cypress waving over them. Its palaces, its tombs, its baths, its temples, stand majestic and solitary amid the waste of time and desolation.

From ancient Rome, turn we now our attention to the time when—

"Joy to the world our Saviour is born."

I find myself descending the very steps our beloved Saviour had descended, a prisoner, over 1,800 years before at Jerusalem.

I stood upon the very steps and peered into the gloom and darkness of the Mamertine Prison, where Paul and Peter were cast, bound in chains.

I was in the very house where St. Paul lived; was in the prison in which he was thrown—saw the very cup with which he baptised.

Filled with a strange reverence and awe, imagination led me back through the dim dark vista of long ages ago, to the days when Paul, standing up before Festus, surrounded by the High Priests and the Jews, appealed to Cæsar as a Roman citizen.

Were it not for this appeal to Cæsar, Rome, for aught we know, might never have became the "Holy City." But Paul, bound in chains, to Rome must go, and from that day to this, the "Eternal City" has been the centre of the most bitter religious controversies the world has ever witnessed. The glimmering dawn looming up from beyond the eastern hills of Bethlehem, its gentle light growing brighter and brighter, gives evidence of a New Era, whose brightness shall penetrate the uttermost parts of the earth.

At 10:30 P. M., I left Rome for Florence by the night express train.

I experienced a terrible night of it, the heat being excessively oppressive, and for the first time during my trip through Italy, found the car crowded and uncomfortable; I essayed to sleep, but with the exception of a few "cap naps," I met with indifferent success.

At 7 A. M., I arrived in the beautiful city of Florence. Its situation is peculiarly happy, in the vale of Arno which forms one continued interchange of garden and grove, enclosed by hills and distant mountains.

Its public buildings are fine, though all modern. Being surpassed by those of Rome, they no longer excite any peculiar interest.

The environs of Florence are nearly as romantic as those of Rome, and whose "Etrurian shades high over-arched embower" has been rendered classical by the immortal verse of Milton, who is supposed to have drawn from it his picture of Paradise, when he describes it—

> "Shade above shade
> A woody theatre of stateliest view."

More remote, and approaching to the greatest height of the Appennines, the sacred hermitage of Camaldoli stands in a valley. Fourteen miles higher up, amid the most solitary and savage recesses of the Appennine Mountains, is the Franciscan Convent of Lavernia, containing 80 friars. It is seated on a lofty rock, broken into numberless pinnacles, while thick groves, rising to the summit and nodding over the steps, cast a rich and mellow shade upon the whole scene.

As the afternoon wore away, I found myself growing quite sick, probably from the constant strain and excitement resting on my nervous system, so returning to my hotel I was advised to keep quiet and seek rest, which I accordingly did. After invigorating exhausted nature with a small medicinal application, I felt somewhat revived, but nevertheless kept quiet until the following morning, when I availed myself of the invitation extended to me from Mr. Tilden of Boston, whose private residence is charmingly situated on the outskirts of Florence ; arriving at his villa I was introduced to his amiable wife and daughter, whom I found to be excellent company and most thoroughly accomplished. From thence, accompanied by my guide, I enjoyed one of the most delightful rides through the surrounding country, which is truly charming.

The next day being Saturday, and as I had got quite enough of sight seeing in the city of Florence, I set out for Venice at 7 P. M., via fast express train.

The morning was serene and beautiful, not a cloud to be seen in the horizon, and a fine car all to myself.

As we pass through the country the scenery is

rich and varied, every foot of which teems with historic interest.

On arriving at the station at Venice, when passing through the entrance, *commissionaires* will be seen who will escort the traveler into the hotel, and a gondolier takes his baggage tickets and procure his baggage.

VIEW IN VENICE.

The city of Venice, "Queen of the Adriatic," is unrivalled as to beauty and situation. It stands on a bay near the Gulf of Venice, built upon 72 islands, with its numberless domes and towers, spires and pinnacles, presenting the appearance of a vast city floating on the bosom of the ocean. The row of magnificent but decaying palaces, which extend along the grand canal, with their light, arabesque balconies and casements, their marble porticoes and peculiar chimneys, present one of the most superb and singular scenes in the world. They stand in majesty of ruin, and exhibit the most affecting combinations of former splendor with present decay ; and as Lord Byron so beautifully expresses it :

" My beautiful, my own
My only Venice—*this is breath !* Thy breeze,

> Thy Adrian sea-breeze, how it fans my face!
> The very winds feel native to my veins,
> And cool them into calmness!"

The most commanding objects are those round the square of St. Mark, the most magnificent public place in Italy. The church of St. Mark rivals in splendor any edifice in that country or in Europe. But this pomp is gloomy and barbaric; the fine domes which swell from its roof, the crowded decorations which cover its porticoes, give it the appearance of an Eastern Pagoda.

The Rialto "where merchants most do congregate," as Shakespeare expresses it, consists of a bold marble arch thrown over the most magnificent part of the great canal, exciting universal admiration.

Ponte de' Sospiri, or "Bridge of Sighs," immortalized by Byron in the fourth canto of Childe Harold :

> "I stood in Venice, on the Bridge of Sighs;
> A palace and a prison on each hand;
> I saw from out the waves her structure rise,
> As from the stroke of the enchanter's wand;
> A thousand years their cloudy wings expand
> Around me, and a dying glory smiles
> O'er the far times, when many a subject land
> Look'd to the winged lion's marble piles,
> Where Venice sat in state, throned on her hundred isles."

Criminals were conveyed across this bridge to hear their sentence, and from there led to their execution ; hence its melancholy but appropriate name.

The Grand Canal, which takes its serpentine course through the city, is intersected by 146 smaller canals, over which there are 306 bridges. The gondola supplies the place of coaches, as carriage or even horseback riding is wholly out of the question here, the streets being so narrow, not usually over 4 or 5 feet wide.

The gondola, is, therefore, the mode of conveyance; it cuts its way so rapidly through the water, that in a short time you may be able to visit every part of the city. They are long, narrow, light vessels, painted black, containing in the centre a cabin nicely fitted up with glass windows, blinds, cushions, &c. Those belonging to private families are much more richly decorated. The price of their hire is four lire per day, and double that price should you wish two rowers. The most pleasant and healthy portion of Venice is in the vicinity of the Grand Canal, which is broad and deep, with magnificent palaces and churches on either side. Venice is a very reasonable place to reside in; rents are low, and living uncommonly cheap; society is pleasant and unrestrained, and foreigners are well received, and usually much pleased.

Sunday, September 1st, I started out at 5:30 A. M., to visit the principal points of interest in the city and its churches, the most important of which is the Church of San Marco; it is built in the form of a Greek cross, and nearly 600 pillars support the decorations inside and out.

The walls of the interior are precious marble; a mosaic of the Virgin of St. Mark is over the central door, and to the right a basin composed of prophyry, supported by a Greek altar, containing holy water.

The altar table in the baptistery is formed from a granite slab, upon which our Saviour is supposed to have stood when he preached to the inhabitants of Tyre, and brought from that city in 1126.

The sacristy, entered by a door at the side of the altar, contains many precious relics, rich jewelry, and a piece of our Saviour's dress.

Gliding along the smooth waters in our gondola, while the sun is going down in picturesque grandeur over the broad waves of the Adriatic, we stop to listen to the boatman's song.

The balmy breeze gently ruffles the deep blue waters as we rock upon its bosom listening, while our oarsman silently keep time with their oars to the song of the Venetian Gondoliers, whom, as we approach, demand a fee, which we cheerfully give.

Twilight steals in upon us, the vesper chimes ring soft and sweet, melt in low cadence on the shore, proclaiming the vesper hour, and we hear the evening hymn to the Virgin borne on the balmy breeze.

At 9 A. M., I left Venice for Milan, passing through a delightful country, whose beautiful scenery rivets the attention of the traveler, bordered all along to our left by the Alps, as far as the eye could reach. I arrived at 3:45 P. M.

MILAN AND THE CATHEDRAL.

Milan is a noble city, situated in a rich plain, watered by the river Po, and is entered by ten gates, the richest one, and the most remarkable, is the Porta Orientale. The city is nearly 8 miles in circumference, and, like most ancient cities, irregularly laid out. It is principally noted for its magnificent cathedral, which astonishes and enchants the beholder.

Fear not that you are expecting more grandeur and beauty than you will realize, for that is impossible.

Its forest of pinnacles, its wilderness of tracery, delicately marked against the grey sky, is constructed entirely of white marble from the quarries of Gandoglia, beyond Lake Maggiore, and the edifice itself is built in the form of a Latin cross, and is said to contain over 4,400 statues.

The roof is reached by ascending a flight of 160 steps, and at sunset, beneath an Italian sky, the view is perfectly magnificent.

> "All its hues
> From the rich sunset to the rising star,
> Their magical variety diffuse ;
> And now they change ; a pale shadow strews
> It's mantle o'er the mountains ; parting day
> Dies like the dolphin, whom each pang imbues
> With a new color as it gasps away,
> The last still loveliest, till—tis gone, and all is grey."

The theatre, Della Scala, is considered the finest in Italy.

At 6:20 I left Milan and arrived at Arona, a small town situated on the borders of one of Italy's fairest lakes, Lake Maggiore, the scenery of which is exquisitely beautiful, that toward the Alps being bold and mountainous, while toward the south it is less steep.

Here I remained over night, retiring early, as I had to catch the first boat in the morning. At 4:30 A. M., I left Arona, via steamer, for a six mile sail on the Lake. I shall never forget the beauty of the scene, as the sun rose, lighting up peak after peak of the glorious Alps, whose summits, crowned with snow, glittered in the resplendent glory of the morning sun. At 6 A. M., I landed at Stresa, where you connect with the diligence which crosses the Alps. I was just in time and fortunate in procuring a good seat. The driver mounts his box, bids the hostler adjust some disarrangement of the harness; the off horse paws the ground impatiently and gives a frightful plunge, which, coming so unexpectedly and sudden, nearly upsets a portly Englishman perched by my side on the top of the diligence, who was then just in the act of lighting a cigar, but failed in the attempt, much to the no small amusement of a congregation of urchins collected by the inn door, who sent up a shout of derisive laughter at his expense.

In the midst of which, crack goes the whip and away we go, leaving the little village and its rustic populace behind us, and rattling over an old moss covered bridge, we begin our ascent of the Alps.

The ascent commences almost immediately after leaving the town, and, passing through green meadows, it approaches the Gorge of Saltine, where the torrent is seen rushing down the valley, amid bristling rocks and rugged embankments.

Passing the First Refuge, a beautiful view of the Rhone Valley is seen; here we breathe our horses and again start off. Two and a half miles the Second Refuge is passed, and pausing for a moment to rest the animals, we obtain another fine view. The road now bends around the valley of the Gauter and crosses the Gauter Bridge, which is so much exposed to avalanches and fearful gusts of wind, that it is left uncovered for fear it would be carried away during the winter storms. Accompanied by my guide I took a short cut and enjoyed the mountain climbing.

ASCENDING THE ALPS WITH MY GUIDE.

The Third Refuge is reached, where fresh post horses are kept. A magnificent view of the valley and the Bernese Alps attracts the attention of the traveler, and arriving at the Fifth Refuge a picture of rugged and barren desolation surrounds the traveler; vegetation has almost ceased, and the eye roams from rock to glacier, while the roaring cataract fills up the picture of rugged and barren grandeur.

From this point to the summit is the most dangerous part of the road. At the Sixth Refuge a cross marks the highest point of the Pass, 6,628 feet above the level of the sea. About half a mile and we reach a place for refreshments, called the *Hospice*, a similar establishment to that of the Great St. Bernard, founded by Napoleon I. Entertainment is gratuitous, but visitors are expected to put as much, if not *more*, into the poor box, than a similar entertainment would cost him in an inn.

Passing the Seventh Refuge we arrive at Sim-

WAGON ROAD OF NAPOLEON.

plon. The road now passes through the *Gallery of Gonda*, the longest tunnel of the Simplon, over 700 feet in length, hewn out of the solid rock. As we pass further on, the Falls of Fressinone dash with its ceaseless roar wildly through the gorge of rocks that rise almost perpendicular to the height of 2,000 feet. Then we pause to get down and view the terrible grandeur of the scene.

> "And you, ye crags, upon whose extreme edge
> I stand, and on the torrents brink beneath
> Behold! the tall pines dwindling into shrubs,
> In dizziness of distance; when a leap,
> A stir, a motion, even a breath, would bring
> My breast upon its rocky bosom's bed
>   To rest forever."

A few moments and we are off again, and at length reach Gondo, the first Swiss village, where an old tower is used for an inn, and beyond a granite column on the left of the road, marks the Italian frontier, which, upon passing, we find ourselves in Switzerland.

Below us the country assumes a new aspect, and we suddenly find ourselves transferred as if by magic, from savage, wild and rugged grandeur, to tressled vines, green chestnuts, gray olives and balmy air.

This celebrated route which we have just crossed has been made memorable for all time from the fact of its having been built under the decree of the Emperor Napoleon I.

After the battle of Marengo, with the bitter experience of his former difficult attempt in crossing the Alps with his army, and the loss of so many of his brave soldiers amid the snows and glaciers of the Alps, he determined to have a great military road to Italy, and ordered the stupendous undertaking to be commenced, which was considered at the time to be one of the greatest achievments of modern engineering skill.

It commenced at Geneva and ended at Milan, and cost about three and a half million of dollars, requiring the labor of over 30,000 men to complete the work.

At 9 P. M., the diligence brought us all safe to Briez, of which we were right heartily glad, being very fatigued with the journey.

As we looked back and saw the Alps bathed in a flood of moonlight, their grandeur seemed even more sublime than if viewed in the day. Briez is a small town of about 800 inhabitants, situated at the base of the Simplon.

At 7.20 next morning I left Briez for Martigny. Never will I forget this delightful railroad ride. It was just after a very hard storm; the atmosphere was pure and delicious, and the scenery bright and glorious; on one side of the railroad flowed a beautiful river, and on the other, a long range of Alpine scenery, from amidst which Mont Blanc could be seen towering above all others.

Peak after peak looming up, crowned with their canopy of eternal snow, reflected their silvery sheen in the bright rays of the morning sun, while around me, Elysian fields, tressled vineyards and the Swiss cottages here and there peeping out from the Alpine mountain heights, painted a picture on my memory akin to that my imagination would portray of Paradise. I was anxious to ascend Mont Blanc, and reaching Martigny at 9.30 A. M., I met with a number of travelers pursuing the journey on foot, preferring to take in the scenery at their leisure, and perhaps, also, on the score of economy. It costs 12 francs for a horse, and 12 francs for a guide, or a carriage can be hired for 40 francs.

As I am not over fond of walking, particularly a distance of 27 miles, and had got tired of horseback riding on my ascent of Mount Vesuvius, I concluded I would hire a wagon.

A party of Englishmen hailing from London,

HOTEL CLERC, MARTIGNY.

and with whom I had taken breakfast, boasted

considerably of their ability of reaching the mountain as soon as I could with my guide and conveyance. I only laughed at their proverbial "blowing," and assured them I would give them two hours start and beat them at that.

So away they started on their journey, a jolly rollicking party, the true typical representatives of Mr. John Bull.

All things being in readiness, and nothing of particular interest to detain me any longer here, I started off for Mont Blanc. The road proceeds in a zig-zag direction, now to the left, then to the right. Now traversing a wild ravine, and up the steep declivity to a Swiss hamlet, which we leave and press onward.

It is 4 P. M. when we reach a roadside inn; our horses are tired, and the guide suggests an hour's stop, to rest and feed the animals, and recuperate our flagging energies.

To this I readily consented, and as I entered the inn my eyes lighted upon my English wor-

ROAD SIDE INN ON THE ALPS.
Here I met the three "Red Noses."

thies, seated around a table discussing the merits of a bottle of champagne, while the formidable array of empty dishes and disordered table plainly indicated that fearful havoc had, in all probability, been made upon sundry chunks of roast beef, a few ribs of which alone were left to tell the tale.

"Hallo, there!" says I.

"Hi, yi! my heyes, is that you," ejaculated one of them, with good round paunch, and a jolly red nose.

"Well, I declare," added his elbow neighbor. "You must have slid down here from some Alpine glacier on the mountains."

"Not a bit of it," replied I.

"You don't know me—always ahead of time—come John—Charley—Henry—or whatever your name is," addressing a diminutive Swiss specimen of humanity who wore a smock coat and a little white apron. "Dance around now, and get me something to eat."

At this my English friends roared out, but I did not catch the joke.

"Ha, say, you'll 'av to warble to 'im in the sweet accents of the Tyrol."

Nothing abashed, and enjoying my newly discovered difficulty, I cried out:

"Cominze here, habinze dinnare for me," with a terrible effort at foreign pronounciation.

Another guffaw burst forth from the throats of the Englishmen.

"That's very good for German," says one. "Now twist your tongue around to a longitude of twenty degrees west of Greenwich, and gently touch it up with a little of the Swiss dialect."

"Give it up," cried I, in despair, and slashing down my slouch hat, I strode for the door and beckoned for my guide.

"You see, gentlemen, there's no use of trying to bluff Beatty; why, six months from now, some of your daughters will be playing away for dear

life on a Beatty Piano in the adjoining parlor."
'My heyes!" retorted our worthy possessor of the red nose. "Perhaps you'll be hoisting one on top of the Pyramids of Egypt next."

"Yes," cried I. "Can't tell gentlemen—can't tell—stranger things than that have happened," saying which, I proceeded to instruct my guide, who could speak English, what I desired, and drawing a chair up to where they were seated, accepted a proffered glass of water, upon receiving which, I rose reverentially as they proposed a toast.

"By hall means, by hall means, Mr. Beetee," cried one.

"The Beatty Piano and Organ for ever, gentlemen," cried another.

They all drank the toast, amid the expostulation of one blink-eyed gentleman to the right, who wheezed out asthmatically.

"To blazes with yer Horgans, let's 'av a toast what is a toast;" saying which, all hands filled up again, and he rose slowly from his seat.

"Gentlemen, 'eres to Hold Hingland;" saying which, they all drank with reverence.

At this juncture my dinner was announced, and I left our worthy Johnny Bulls to continue their convivial repast, while I adjourned to an inner apartment, free from the noise and bustle of the inn, and where it was more congenial to my own taste. As I gazed out of my tressled window the magnificence of the scenery was truly enchanting. Hundreds of feet below I espy the winding silver thread of what appears to be a little meandering brook, but which in reality is a wide flowing river, and down in the valley clustering houses and a church nestled and half concealed amid foliage and jutting promontories of mossy rocks.

Above me, still further, the glaciers of the Alps look down upon me in their majesty, as though laughing at the feeble efforts of man to scale their dizzy heights. From my window I discern my English friends walking up the road at a brisk pace, and laughing heartily among themselves.

The hour of respite having expired, I am again seated in my conveyance ready to pursue my journey, but this time I have a companion, a beautiful young lady, for whom my host has interceded, and of course I accede, as it adds additional interest to have so agreeable a companion with whom I could converse, interchange ideas, and enjoy, with mutual admiration, the scenery before us.

On leaving the inn, the road clings close to the mountain, and further on we pass through a dark tunnel, from which emerging, and urging on our horses, we soon overtake our English travellers, and exchanging salutations, we pass on, soon leaving them far in the distance. Now the road takes a turn, crosses a rustic bridge over a swift cataract that roars and plunges down a steep precipice and is lost sight of amid the shrubs, boulders and pines of the rugged mountain, and a village beyond over which seems to hang, as it were, huge mountains of ice and snow, as though a breath might cause it to break away and descending in one swift avalanche, spread ruin and devastation before it, At this point we leave our horses and proceed with our guide on foot.

At length, by 8.30 we reach

CHAMOUNIX.

This lovely retreat, once so secluded and almost unknown, is now the favorite resort, and rivals Niagara or Saratoga in all the excitement and bustle of a favorite summer resort.

After paying and dismissing my guide and

conveyance I repaired to my hotel, located in a beautiful portion of the town, fully satisfied with my journey from Martiney to Chamounix. Having rested for an hour or so and partaken of some refreshments, I again sally forth—and whom should I encounter but my portly friend with the red nose and his three English companions, who, decidedly tired, weary, and foot sore, were sorry, I warrant, for not taking my advice and hiring a conveyance. The next morning I awoke full of enthusiasm, eager for fresh ventures. From the windows of the hotel I could obtain a splendid view of Mont Blanc, and with the aid of a powerful telescope could even discern people ascending its steep sides, bound for its ice-capped summit.

At 7.30 I have decided to ascend "Mer de Glace"—the sea of ice—which I had viewed from the top of Mount Blanc the previous day; so procuring me a fresh guide and a mule, away we go, in company with a celebrated physician of Boston and some twenty ladies and gentlemen, all bent on the same journey.

Oo, on, on, we go up the mountain side, our mules first on one side then on the other; now near the edge of some dangerous precipice, from which I would turn my head in dizziness, and again hugging close to the rocky boulders that jut out as though to intercept us on our path. The Doctor was mounted on a splendid animal—all white, and named Mont Blanc. He was a fine leader, and nothing could induce him to go but just so fast.

"Now, Mont Blanc," says the Doctor, addressing his mule, "you are a noble animal, you have not stumbled once. I have great confidence in you—see that you keep up your reputation."

And the dumb brute, as though conscious of the compliment paid him, pricked up his ears and jogged along with a sure and steady gait.

From the height of Montauvert we saw the Mer de Glace shining in the morning sun, and saw a party crossing on the other side.

In half an hour more we found ourselves cross-

MER DE GLACE OR SEA OF ICE.

ing the Mer de Glace, and were delighted at the extraordinary spectacle presented. At the place where we stood, the pressure from the snow above had caused the ice to mass itself together in heaps, and to assume the most remarkable shapes; grotesque forms of ice, irregular and jagged, piled up one above another, bearing a resemblance to transparent towers, and again like so many ice witches and hobgoblins huddled together in wild fantastic groups, with here and there some lofty column looming up, followed by a long range, like the broken and dismantled ramparts of some ruined city, while some giant shaft of ice looming over the rest suddenly disappears under the magic wand of the sun's warm rays and toppling over is precipitated into the abyss below with a roar resembling subterranean thunder.

At 3.15 P. M., I find myself safe back to my hotel. In the evening I took a stroll out into the streets of this old and picturesque town, but retired early, as at 7 A. M. the next morning I set out for Geneva. All along from Chamounix to Geneva an extended panorama of the Alps presents itself, and from amid its long extended range lifts the snow capped peaks of Mont Blanc.

Now, the ascent becomes extremely difficult so clutching the rope tied to my guide's side, with a tighter hold, and planting my pole into the crust of snow, I began the more difficult part of my laborious journey. One runs the continual danger of slipping and falling while climbing over the icy billows, and occasionally finding oneself upon the brink of a wide crevice in a mass of ice two or three hundred feet deep, across which one must leap, without any other foothold than a smooth icy wave or hillock. As I looked down the broad fissures and yawning chasms, I felt as though I could go no further; my guide encouraged me with the assurance that we had passed the most difficult part, but I found it no easy task climbing alongside of a perpendicular rock, without anything to hold on to but the rope from my guide, following a narrow ledge cut in the rocks, midway between two perpendicular walls, the one above me and the other below, from which dizzy height I see the Mer-de-Glace dazzling my eyes with its bright reflections.

The guide now advised me to hasten, because the stones were being frequently precipitated from the rocks above, and should they clog our narrow pathway where one can scarcely turn, or should even a gust of wind come howling down the steep declivity, we would be plunged in the frightful depths below. Above me I gaze with terror upon the heavy masses of rock hanging over my head, as they appeared just ready to fall. "Nay! on! on! cries the guide, as he pulls my slipping feet up the crumbling debris, and I inwardly pray for deliverance from what would be certain death should I falter. A few minutes

HOTEL NEAR THE SEA OF ICE.

more, and we reach the summit. I felt unspeakably thankful that I had overcome the dangers that had surrounded me on every side. The sinking sun lit up the snow-capped peaks in the gold and purple grandeur of the dying day. Mont Blanc and the Col de Balme vied with each other in their majestic splendor, standing forth in all their grand and silent sublimity, whose very silence proclaims from generation to generation, the glory, greatnes, and majesty of our great Creator. The descent, though less toilsome, is still dangerous; so slowly and carefully picking our way down the rugged rocks, jumping deep chasms, and toiling through the snow and ice we finally reach our horses, which mounting, we travel over another fearful road, washed out by the late storm, and commence our descent considerably faster than we went up.

Some conception of its immense height can be had viewed from this distance. The view of the Alps, however, from this point is rather tame compared to the Simplon Pass route.

At 2 P. M. I arrived at Geneva. The next morning, "at early peep o' day," the day bidding fair to be fine, I was up and enjoyed a fine walk on the shores of the beautiful Lake of Geneva.

My French money, with which I had provided myself in London, now gave out, and part of the day was consumed in arranging my financial affairs, and purchasing my tickets for Germany, Belgium, and Holland.

I had already secured my ticket from Geneva back to Paris before leaving France for Italy, but this I could sell again, and so I determined to extend my travels through Germany.

Having arranged my plans accordingly, I continued my tour of inspection.

Geneva is beautifully situated at the southern extremity of Lake Geneva. The river Rhone divides the city into two parts, and is connected by six bridges.

HOTEL DE LA MATROPOLE, GENEVA.

As you drive on the left side of the lake you pass Diodati, the villa of Lord Byron during his residence in Switzerland in 1816. It was called after a friend of the poet, who visited him here. During his residence here, it is said he composed his tragedy of Manfred, and his third Canto of Childe Harold.

Near the lake is the villa of Sir Robert Peel, and another formerly occupied by the Empress Josephine.

On the road to Chateau Rothschild, about $4\frac{1}{2}$ miles from Geneva is Ferney, which contains the chateau formerly occupied by Voltaire, the great French Infidel, whose writings have cursed the earth with their false doctrines.

At 11 A. M. (of the next day), I departed for Berne, the capital of Switzerland. It stands in a beautiful position on the left bank of the river Aar. The town derives its name from Bären, the German for bears, that being the figure or emblem on there crests and armorials bearings of the Canton.

The natives of Berne worship bears much the same as the natives of Constantinople worships pidgeons, or the natives of Egypt are said to worships cats. For many centuries numerous bears were kept at the expense of the city, and a certain fund is now devoted for that purpose.

The principal building is the Cathedral, which contains one of the largest organs in the world, upon which I heard "The Storm at Sea," performed by their celebrated organist, and which was truly impressive and grand. From the old cemetery of the cathedral, covered with fine shady trees, from an elevation of over 100 feet above the river, a splendid view of Berne can always be had.

Having seen all of interest in this city, I left at 6 A. M., the next day for Frankfort-on-the-Main.

Arriving at Basle, our baggage is again overhauled by the government officials. A very singular custom prevails in this city—that of keeping their clocks one hour in advance of those in other cities; one reason given for the curious practice is that the attempt of an enemy to surprise the city was defeated by the town clock striking one instead of twelve; the conspirators in the town thinking they were an hour too late, failed to keep their appointment. The citizens ever after kept their clocks an hour ahead of time. From here we proceed on our journey to Heidelberg. It is one of the principal towns of Baden, and contains 20,100 inhabitants, one-third of whom are Catholics. The principal point of interest is the Castle of Heidelberg, founded in the 14th century, which combines the double character of palace and fortress. The cellars of the Castle are very extensive, capable of holding 800 hogsheads of wine. In front of the Castle is a wooden statue of the Court fool, Porkes, who never went to bed sober, and always on a short allowance of from 15 to 18 bottles daily. From the terrace and garden most magnificent views may be obtaiued.

COURT YARD, HEIDELBERG CASTLE.

The Church of the Holy Ghost is a singular building, divided in the centre by a partition running the whole length of the church, and the two services, Catholic and Protestant, are performed under the same roof.

The University of Heidelberg is one of the most celebrated, and ranks equal with Vienna and Prague. From here we proceed to Frankfort-on-the-Main, which we reach at 8.30 P. M.

This city is one of the most ancient; Charlamagne had a palace here, and held a council within its walls in 794, and a century later it became the capital of Germany. It is the native place of Rothschild, the richest banker in the world. The house where he was born, No. 148 Judengasse (Jews Street) is still shown.

The Cathedral is an ancient edifice, commenced in the 13th century.

Outside of the Friedberg gate is situated the colossal mass of granite rocks grouped together in memory of the Hessians who fell defending Frankfort, the whole surmounted by a military device taken from the French. It was erected by the king of Prussia.

In front of the theatre (a very fair one) is a monumental statue, erected to Germany's most celebrated poet—Goethe.

The house where he was born is situated at No. 74 in the Hirschgraben, and his father's coat of arms—*three lyres*—over the door.

A magnificent bronze statue of Schiller, the poet, was erected on Schillerplatz in 1864.

The monument to *Guttenberg*, the inventor of printing, is situated on the Ross Markt.

The central figure, with the types in his left hand is Guttenberg, on his right stands Faust and on his left Schöffer. The home of Martin Luther is situated in the Domplatz, the greatest leader in the Reformation, and to whom the world is indebted for the Protestant Religion freed from the superstition of the dark ages.

The ancient fortifications have been converted into public gardens, which are one of the greatest attractions in the city.

At 7 A. M. I left Frankfort for Mayence, which is a city of great antiquity. It was founded by Drusus 14 years B. C.

Among the principal edifices of Mayence which are of great antiquity, is the Cathedral, a vast pile of red sandstone, began in the tenth and finished in the eleventh century. A site formerly occupied by the dwelling house of Guttenberg, the inventor of printing, a native of the town, is seen with interest.

At 9.20 A. M. I stepped on board the steamer for a sail down the river Rhine to Cologne.

It happened very fortunate for me that this steamer, one of the fastest in Europe, was used as an express between Mayence and Cologne, a distance of 117 miles, as it makes only two stops on the way. On taking a way boat, one must make at least 30 stops. The passage down the river Rhine is replete with interest, being the most picturesque river in the world.

Here one sees clustering vineyards covering steep and shore, and interlacing the most romantic ruins. Nowhere is the vine cultivated to a greater extent. The humblest peasant has his square yard of vineyard, and every accessible spot is covered with this favorite plant.

The well-known "Hock" wine, erroneously applied to all German wines, is grown eastward of Mayence.

As we pass the Seven Sisters a heavy thunder storm sprang up, which lasted but a short time, however, as the sun soon shone out as bright as ever, and the foliage on either side brightened into a deeper emerald, and added to the charm of the scene.

As we pass down the Rhine, the ruins of Ehrenfels rise in the distance beyond, immortalized by the celebrated poet, Southey, in the following tradition :

"The summer and autumn hath been so wet,
That in winter the corn was growing yet ;
'Twas a piteous sight, to see all around
The grain lie rotting on the ground.

Every day the starving poor
Crowded around Bishop Hatto's door,
For he had a plentiful last year's store ;
And all the neighborhood could tell
His granaries were furnish'd well.

At last Bishop Hatto appointed a day
To quiet the poor without delay ;
He bade them to his great barn repair,
And they should have food for the winter there.

Rejoiced at such tidings, good to hear,
The poor folk flock'd from far and near ;
The great barn was full as it could hold
Of women and children, and young and old.

Then when he saw it could hold no more,
Bishop Hatto he made fast the door ;
And while for mercy on Christ they call,
He set fire to the barn and burnt them all.

'I' faith 'tis an excellent bonfire !' quote he,
'And the country is greatly obliged to me
For ridding it, in these times forlorn,
Of rats that only consume the corn.'

So then to the palace returned he,
And he sat down to his supper merrily ;
And he slept that night like an innocent man,
But Bishop Hatto never slept again.

In the morning, as he entered the hall,
Where his picture hung against the wall,
A sweat like death all o'er him came,
For the rats had eaten it out of the frame.

As he look'd, there came a man from his farm,
He had a countenance white with alarm,
'My lord, I opened your granaries this morn,
And the rats had eaten all your corn.'

Another came running presently,
And he was as pale as pale could be ;
'Fly, my lord bishop, fly,' quoth he,
'Ten thousand rats are coming this way,
The Lord forgive you for yesterday !'

'I'll go to my tower on the Rhine,' replied he ;
' 'Tis the safest place in all Germany ;
The walls are high, and the shores are steep,
And the stream is strong and the waters deep.'

Bishop Hatto fearfully hasten'd away,
And he crossed the Rhine without delay
And reach'd his tower, and barred with care
All the windows, doors, and loop holes there.

He laid him down, and closed his eyes;
But soon a scream made him arise;
He started and saw two eyes of flame
On his pillow, from whence the screaming came.

He listened and look'd: it was only the cat,
But the Bishop he grew more fearful for that;
For she sat screaming, mad with fear,
At the army of rats that were drawing near.

For they have swum over the river so deep,
And they have climbed the shores so steep,
And now by thousands up they crawl
To the holes and windows in the wall.

Down on his knees the Bishop fell,
And faster and faster his beads did he tell
As louder and louder, drawing near
The saw of their teeth without he could hear.

And in at the windows, and in at the door,
And through the walls by thousands they pour,
And down through the ceiling, and up through the
    floor,
From the right and the left, from behind and before,
From within and without, from above and below—
And all at once to the Bishop they go.

They have whetted their teeth against the stones,
And now they pick the Bishop's bones;
They gnaw'd the flesh from every limb,
For they were sent to do judgment on him,"

At 4.20 P. M. I arrived at Cologne. It is the third city in the Prussian kingdom. It is built in the form of a crescent close by the borders of

COLOGNE, PRUSSIA.

the river Rhine, and strongly fortified, the walls forming a circuit of nearly seven miles.

The chief glory of Cologne is its magnificent Cathedral, which is one of the finest specimens of Gothic architecture in the world. Although commenced in the year 1248, it is still unfinished; nearly $2,000,000 have been expended on it by the kings of Prussia during the last 40 years. Behind the high altar is the Chapel of the Magi, or the three kings of Cologne.

It contains the bones of the three wise men of the east, who journeyed to Bethlehem bearing presents to the infant Christ. The skulls of the Magi, crowned with diamonds, with their names written in rubies. Among the numerous relics in the sacristy is a bone of St. Matthew.

The Church of St. Ursula is one of the most remarkable sights in this city. The tradition runs, that St. Ursula, daughter to the King of Brittany, accompanied by 11,000 virgins, ascended the Rhine, on their pilgrimage to the Holy City. On their return the whole party was barbarously murdered by the Huns because they refused to break their vows of chastity, and the bones of all the attendant virgins were gathered together, and the present church erected to contain them.

In every direction these hideous relics stare you in the face. St. Ursula herself is exhibited in a coffin, which is surrounded by the skulls of a few of her favorite attendants. The room in which she is laid also contains many other relics, among these are the chains with which St. Peter was bound, and one of the clay vessels used by the Saviour at the marriage of Cana.

The well-known perfume, Eau de Cologne, is manufactured here, and is exported in large quantities. My impressions were not very favorable, from the fact that there does not appear to be any regard for the Sabbath day.

Monday, Sept. 9th, at 9 A. M., I left Cologne for Brussels, the capital of Belgium, and beautifully situated on the river Senne, about 50 miles from the sea. The fortifications of a century ago have all been removed, and on their site beautiful boulevards and promenades have been made, planted with stately linden trees, extending nearly five miles around the city. Four principal streets surround the park or palace garden, any of which it is difficult to surpass in any city in Europe, the *tout ensemble* of the whole being truly charming. The Rue Bellevue containing the King's palace, the Rue Ducale, in which is the palace of the Prince of Orange (the late King of Holland), the Rue Brabant and the Rue Royale, on which are situated the finest mansions in Brussels; in fact the whole city, opera houses, theatres, squares, restaurants and cafes, is a miniature Paris.

Brussels contains several splendid Cathedrals, erected in the middle ages.

The Cathedral of St. Gudale, is surmounted by

two large square towers, from the top of which Antwerp is distinctly seen. The pulpit of the Cathedral is formed of wonderfully carved groups of figures representing the expulsion of Adam and Eve from Paradise; the figures are the size of life. The organ is remarkable for its depth and power of intonations and perfect unison.

On a visit to the old palace the finest pictures in the world are on exhibition, principally Reubens and Corregios. The battle field of Waterloo, is 12 miles from the city. The field is now covered with smiling corn, a conical mound 200 feet in height, and surmounted by a bronze figure of the Belgic lion, commemorates the events of June, 1815, when Napoleon Bonaparte with a force of 70,000 men confronted an English army of 140,000 men and 380 pieces of cannon, under the Duke of Wellington. Out of thirteen of the greatest pitched battles recorded in history, Napolean lost but two, the most unfortunate of which was fought here—the Battle of Waterloo.

The next day I paid a visit to the old palace, situated near the Palais Royale. It was built in 1300 and rebuilt in 1746. It now contains museums, public libraries, galleries of paintings and sculpture, and a lecture-room.

In the picture gallery there are some very fine paintings, especially those purchased by the City at the King of Holland's sale, and are the finest I ever inspected.

One of the most novel scenes that I witnessed while gazing from the steeple of the Hotel de Ville, was whole troops of dogs harnessed to small carts, driven by peasant women, who, at that early hour in the morning, come in from the adjacent country with their loads of farm truck, trudging along to market by the side of their canine teams. Such a yelping and barking as some of them set up, mingled with the hooting of boys and scolding women. While some of these trained dogs, long inured to toil, seemed more sober than the rest; looking neither to right

STREET SCENE.

or left, they wear an air of responsibility, as if they had more at stake than their masters.

At 2.30, I left Brussels for Antwerp, and as the distance is not great, arrived there in an hour. Antwerp, situated on the right bank of the Scheldt, is the chief port of Belgium. There are few places in Europe so rich in magnificent churches, and embellished by the most remarkable works of art, such as Reubens', Van Dyke's, Jordaen's and other great masters of painting, who were natives of Antwerp. The principal street, Place de Mére, rivals any in Europe.

Nothing of particular interest attracting my attention here, I took train for Rotterdam. The town contains many charitable institutions, the central prison of the Netherlands, and many superior schools. Erasmus, the Reformer, was born here in 1467. The house of his birth is still preserved.

* * * * * * *

From here we take steamer to Queensboro, where at 6.25 the next morning we arrive,

Here we are obliged to submit to our baggage being overhauled previous to our trip to London, where we arrived safe and sound once more, having made the complete tour of the Continent in as short a space of time as it was possible, compatible with ease and comfort.

Here I am again in the great British metropolis, safely esconced at the Hotel Midland, where, after recuperating exhausted nature by a good rest, I concluded to give the City my entire attention before embarking for America.

THAMES, LONDON.

London, the home of our illustrious ancestors. Men of mighty genius, who have left their imperishable and stupendous works behind them to enrich the coming ages with their wealth of architecture, science and art, palaces, cathedrals, towers and spires, hoary with age and enshrined in traditions. My first sally was to

WESTMINSTER ABBEY.

> "That antique pile, behold,
> Where royal heads receive the sacred gold ;
> It gives them crowns, and does their ashes keep.
> There, made like Gods, like mortals there they sleep,
> Making the circle of their reign complete—
> These suns of Empire, where they rise they set."

This venerable pile, founded by one of the early Saxon kings, passing through all the vicissitudes of time, and ravages of war, still retains its ancient grandeur. In this building the coronation of the Kings and Queens of England have been held. An attempt to describe all the historical relics, points of interest, and traditions attached to each, would fill volumes. The Poet's Corner, contains the monuments of Shakespeare, Milton, Addison, Sheridan, Garrick and many others. Its chapels, aisles and transepts are all filled whit monuments erected to England's brightest intellects, commemorative of their departed worth.

It is with feelings of reverential awe that I passed through this venerable Cathedral, and gazed upon the sarcophagus containing the bones of Henry V., and his brother Richard, Duke of York, who were murdered by their cruel uncle Richard III, and passed on to the magnificent monument to the memory of Queen Elizabeth, and from there to the tomb of Anne, Queen of Denmark, and Henry, Prince of Wales.

But turning from the splendid tombs of kings, princes and the nobility, I approach the plain and simple statue of John Wesley, the founder of Methodism, sculptured in pure marble, and placed upon a pedestal of Peterhead granite ; I read engraved thereon :

> "The best of all is,
> God is with us."

which was one of the last utterances of this distinguished divine, whom Southey, the poet laureate of England in those days, considered one of the greatest and purest of men.

"A greater poet may rise than Homer or Milton, a greater theologian than Calvin, a greater philosopher than Bacon, a greater dramatist than any of ancient or modern fame, but a more distinguished revivalist of the churches than John Wesley, never."

Amid all the pomp and splendor of sculptured marble that everywhere met my gaze in this grand old cathedral, none impressed itself upon my mind more than John Wesley's, because he was one of the principal architects that God used in the erection of that temple which is to be "built without hands" in the city of our God, and which will live ages upon ages after the earth shall have crumbled away, and be no more forever.

From Westminster I visited the Aquarium, and in the evening the Princes' Theatre, where I witnessed the representation of "Uncle Tom's Cabin," making me feel as though I was once more in America.

The morning came, and with it the usual London fog. I was quite sick, and the dullness of the morning was in harmony with my feelings; but reflecting that the time for my travels in foreign lands was fast drawing to a close, I concluded to shake off my sickness, and remembering the suggestion of Mr. Douglass at my home office, to visit the Crystal Palace, I set out for the same, provided myself with the necessary piece of pasteboard from the box-office of the Underground Railroad, after paying the stipulated charge thereon, and betook myself to the cars, wherein I experienced my first sensation in riding through an underground railroad tunnel. Shut out from the world above, and with but little, if anything, to attract my attention in my subterraneous trip, I can't say I was particularly pleased, save that it was an expeditious way of arriving at my destination. I soon found myself viewing the wonders of nature and art under the brilliant dome of the Crystal Palace, but having viewed objects of interest to a greater extent in the Paris Exposition, I was not long in passing through its various departments.

It occurred to me to visit Alexander Palace, but the ride occupies nearly an hour, and I was meditating whether I would attempt the journey, when the sight, however, of 500 sweet little orphan children singing the sweet songs of Zion, led me to decide upon going, and which I afterwards found well repaid me for my trouble.

I left the Midland Grand Hotel next day, and located at the Viaduct Hotel, it being more central, while the former I found too far on one side of the city.

St. Paul's Cathedral next demanded my attention, which is situated in the most central part of the metropolis. It stands on an elevated position at the end of Ludgate Hill, and its lofty dome may be seen for miles around. The magnificent deep tones of its great bell, which is only tolled on the occasion of a death in the royal family, can be heard far out of the city.

Here rest the remains of the Duke of Wellington, Sir Joshua Reynolds, and Admiral Nelson, whose motto, "Never give up the Ship," will ever be remembered.

The choir is extremely beautiful, and rich in magnificent carvings.

The next day I thought I would pay a visit to some of the English advertising agencies, for where one spends such large amounts of money in advertising, as is required in my business, it was a matter of special interest to me to understand the English mode of transacting this class of business, and how it compared with the American system, in connection with which I visited the principal daily papers in London, amply repaid me for my trouble, winding up my expedition with a steamboat ride on the Thames, with which I was well pleased.

Sunday I repaired to the Rev. Mr. Spurgeon's church, and heard him preach. The text was taken from Matthew 1st chap., and 21st verse.

I was much pleased and edified by his sermon, and am not surprised that he won such a wide and well merited fame, both at home and abroad.

Avoiding all efforts at a splendid flow of language, or to dress up his discourse in the flowery rhetoric of the day, but in good old homespun English he drove the truth into the hearts of his hearers, with a power and energy which I plainly could see was the main fulcrum on which his great reputation rested.

The evening set in with every indication of a storm, so I remained indoors, and spent my time in meditating over the traits and characteristics of the people with whom I found myself surrounded.

I must say that I am well and favorably impressed with the English; their reverence for God's holy day, throughout the length and the breadth of the land, struck me forcibly as compared with the observance of the day in other countries through which I had just travelled.

Very little rain fell although the sky looked so threatening, but I afterwards learnt from the daily papers that a severe storm had passed over England and Scotland, causing immense destruction of life and property.

Monday I repaired to the ticket office, procured me a ticket for Glasgow, via Edinburgh. I left London, via the Midland Railway, on Scot's fast express, and found myself dashing through old

England at the rate of 70 miles per hour. I must confess the train travelled fast enough for me, as we went rattling and whizzing along, and although in an imported American Pullman Palace Car, I found it difficult to keep my seat. At length we came to a different set or style of fences and land-

SCOTT'S MONUMENT, EDINBURGH.

marks, which plainly indicated we had passed into another country, while the scenery became

decidedly Scottish in its character. 9 P. M., found
our fast express train puffing into the suburbs of
Edinburgh, and it was not long before I found
myself booked for the Hotel Royal, just opposite
Sir Walter Scott's monument. Tired and weary
with my days travel I retired, intent upon getting
a good nights sleep, preparatory to my morning
perambulations.

Edinburgh, the capital of Scotland, is situated
on two ridges of hills within two miles of the
Firth of Forth.

Through its centre a deep wild and rocky ravine extends, dividing the city into the old and new town, and on the summit of a tremendous precipice stands

EDINBURGH CASTLE.

> There watching high the least alarm
> Thy rough rude fortress gleams afar;
> Like some bold vet'ran, gray in arms
> And marked with many a seamy scar;
> Thy pond'rous wall and massy bar,
> Grim-rising o'er the rugged rock,
> Have oft withstood assailing war,
> And oft repelled the invader's shock.

This castle teems with romantic interest, and the Crown Jewels are kept deposited here. The next point of interest is the remains of the Palace of Holyrood. It was a magnificent building in former days; the ancient residence of Scottish royalty. The most interesting rooms in the palace are those last occupied by the unfortunate Mary; and where her secretary Rizzio was murdred, the marks of his blood are still to be seen on the floor.

Grayfriar's Church and churchyard is replete with interest. The Martyrs' Monument contains the following inscription: "From May 27, 1661, that the most noble Marquis of Argyle was beheaded, to the 17th of February, 1688, that Mr.

James Renwick suffered, were one way or other murdered and destroyed for the same cause about 18,000; of whom were executed at Edinburgh about one hundred of noblemen, gentlemen, ministers and others, noble martyrs for Jesus Christ."

A ride through the Queen's Drive well repaid me, and beyond are Salisbury's Craigs.

At 8 A. M. the following morning I took the fast express for Glasgow.

VIEW OF GLASGOW, SCOTLAND.

The first and most prominent object which attracts our attention is the Cathedral, which I think ranks next to Westminster Abbey. It is situated in a most picturesque position, and in its church yard, which rises terrace above terrace in the back ground, is erected upon its highest elevation, placed on the top of a fine Doric column, the statue of John Knox, the great Reformer, which looks down upon the dust of those who, laid forever in their narrow cell, sleep the sleep that knows no waking, till the trumpet of the ressurection morn shall rouse them from their lowly bed.

St. George's Square at the terminus of the Edinburgh and Glasgow Railway, is the principal square in the city. It contains the monument of Sir Walter Scott, Sir John Moore, James Watt, Sir Robert Peel, and Lord Clyde.

In the immediate vicinity of the Museum stands the Stewart Memorial Fountain, which commemorates the introduction of Loch Katrine water into Glasgow. On the summit of the fountain there is a beautiful figure of "The Lady of the Lake."

Steam street cars are used to a great extent in this city, and in some of the principal thoroughfares entirely supersede the horse cars.

At 2 P. M. I left Glasgow for Liverpool, traveling through a land which bespoke the thrift and prosperity of its people; passing several beautiful English lakes on my right, as we dash with lightning speed over the rails bound for the great commercial port of Liverpool.

It is the second city in the kingdom, contains about 500,000 inhabitants, and noted for its extensive docks, which are constructed on a most stupendous scale, covering, with the dry-docks, 200 acres, with 15 miles of quays. In the square at the Exchange, is a monument of bronze in honor of Admiral Nelson, representing the dying hero receiving a naval crown of victory, and an enemy crushed and prostrate at his feet. The Derby Museum well repaid me for my visit, but my time was limited, being compelled to arrange the next day for my departure for America.

The next day, Thursday Sept. 19th, at 2.10 P.M. found me on board the steamship City of Richmond, [one of the finest as well as the largest steamers in the world. We had about 700 on board in all, among whom were two Japanese. From Liverpool to Queenstown the sea was very fine; arriving at Queenstown, we were delayed five hours waiting for the mail, which I improved by going on shore to while away time on dry land, knowing well enough, that once my foot trod the deck, I should not have the pleasure of again being on *terra firma* for some time to come. which, though comparatively short, was to me. out on the broad expanse of ocean, long enough, I assure you.

But time crept on, 4 o'clock arrived and all things being in readiness, the last tearful benediction pronounced from parting relatives and friends, and "all aboard" was the warning signal. A few brief moments the bell in the engineer's room rang out, and the monster wheels slowly turning, swung the vessel from her moorings, and away we go, bound for

"The land of the free, and the home of the brave."

Saturday, September 21st, I awoke experiencing a certain squirmishness which gradually grew worse. A rough sea and strong head winds caused the vessel to tumble considerably, and with the exception of, perhaps, six persons, all on board where enjoying the privilege of being seasick. As for me, I kept my bed all day and could not eat a mouthful.

Sunday came and went, but I was still too sick ta leave my berth. The Church of England service was held on board, but I contented myself by remaining in my berth, diverted my mind from things terrestrial to things celestial by reading one of Dr. Spurgeon's fine sermons, together with selected passages from the Bible, and thus I worshipped God on the mighty deep, feeling that I was still preserved in the hollow of His hand and that His mercy still upheld me in all my wanderings through foreign lands.

Monday, September 23d, although cloudy, the sea was considerably smoother, and nearly all on board, including myself, had recovered from their sea-sickness, and were up on deck. The steamer was making good time, with a fine running sea. The evening closed with sacred song, and the next day we experienced a rougher time of it, as a strong head wind was blowing, and the waves heaved and tossed our vessel considerably, bringing back the customary sea-sickness, which I was fortunate enough to be entirely free from on my trip out.

"We'll have a rough night of it," says one of the sailors to me, which assurance was not very comforting, and I mentally braced myself up to the prospect before me.

As the hours grew on, and darkness came brooding over the face of the deep, the wind rushed through the riggiug like the sighing of lost spirits, and the waves rose mountains high. Of a sudden I heard the bell signal for the engines to stop, and full of misgivings and dim forebodings I tumbled out of my berth, or rather I might say some monstrous wave performed the operation for me, as I found myself sprawling out on the floor, trying to hold on to some object of security as I groped my way along, meeting others in like predicament, all wanting to know what the matter was.

"Don't be alarmed," cried a stalwart sailor, "this is a noble vessel, the best that ever rode the waves, and it is almost impossible to wreck her." Wiih this morsel of quieting assurance we waited patiently, all sleep banished and longing for the morning light.

Three and a half long weary hours—they seemed an age to me, as we danced like a feather at the mercy of the sea, lashed into fury by the howling winds, which like so many infuriated demons whirled about our devoted ship as though bidding the angry billows engulph us in its deep, unfathomable depths.

The morning broke at last, but very cold; strong headwinds still prevailed, we had drifted out of our course, and back towards the Irish coast, 8 miles. The sea looked like snowbanks, with its myriad waves lashed into foam, while in the very fury of the elements I could see the goodness and glory of God, whom I felt was with me through storm and sunshine. In the offing we discerned the steamer City of Berlin, bound for Liverpool.

While sitting in the saloon of the steamer, after my severe sea-sickness, I was introduced to a charming young lady—Miss Maggie B. McDonald, of St. Louis, Mo., who, with her brother, was returning from an extended European tour. I found her a most intellectual conversationalist, and an agreeable young lady.

Thursday, September 26th —On board the steamer just one week.

The day is fine and clear, the sea is calm, and its long rolling billows smooth and unbroken, look so innocent and harmless, that a few short hours before were lashed into madness and fury. How gentle, and yet how treacherous, for a few brief hours and again, perhaps, they would be ready to swallow us up in some hidden maelstrom of destruction. We are making splendid time and are nearing the banks of Newfoundland, as it grows colder and colder.

Friday, September 27th.—I had a splendid view of the sun as it peeped out of the east and lit up the wide and mighty ocean with its amber and gold, and the myriad waves far off in the eastern horizon glittered in golden scintillations, which grew in intensity as the God of day rose out of his watery palace, while thousands upon thousands of tiny waves, danced with delight beneath his bright and glorious beams. The birth of another day—another leaf in the great book of eterdity.

At 10 rain set in, but cleared away by 4, and set in extremely cold, with heavy north west winds; at 8 o'clock we are making fine time and through a smooth sea, about 14 knots per hour.

We had a fine concert in the evening, and took up a collection for the Yellow Fever sufferers. Result £20 10s. 8d.

Saturday, Sept. 28, was clear but very cold, with northwest wind and heavy sea. We are making good speed; for the first time since quitting Liverpool, we had a chance to raise our sails. We are expecting to reach New York by to-morrow 2 P. M. All well and hopeful.

Sunday, Sept. 29.—"Land! Land!" these were the magic words that greeted my ears when I awoke, and sure enough upon looking out of the port hole, I could plainly discern the shore of Long Island. All on board are happy, and one of our Japanese passengers kindly favors me with his card—Seigo Tamagawa, Tokio, Japan. He was a Brigadier General, sent by his government to the Paris Exposition, and who also occupied the position of Minister Plenipotentiary to the United States.

Asking the proud purser if he had a tag to place upon my luggage, he in a very rough way replied: "No, I have not."

Which strongly contrasted with our captain, who was found to be a very polite and christian gentleman, knowing no distinction between rich or poor, with a pleasant smile and word for all.

The pilot got on board about two o'clock in the morning, bringing us copies of the New York *Herald*, which were read with intense pleasure, although 3 days old.

Descending to my berth to arrange for my departure, and looking out of the port hole I could see Coney Island and Manhattan Beach, which brought to my mind pleasant recollections of former days.

In the midst of all this bustle and confusion we do not forget that it is God's holy day, and all join in devotional service, and

> "Give God the praise,
> From whom all blessings flow."

At 1 P. M. we pass Sandy Hook. Coming up the bay, we transferred our mail bags to a tug that came alongside, took on a physician, also Mr. England, publisher of the New York *Sun*, and my old friend Crockett, of the Grand Central Hotel.

The first one to greet me on my stepping foot once more on land was my brother Mansfield, who, in company with my excellent financial manager, Mr.——— and my worthy mailing clerk, were all delighted and happy to see me. Entering the carriage my friends had provided, in anticipation of my arrival, we drove rapidly up Broadway to the Grand Central Hotel, where I found a multitude of acquaintances and friends ready to receive me, and to congratulate me upon my safe arrival. At 7 P. M. I was called on by a distinguished New York piano maker, and was met by a hearty reception, and on my return to the hotel, found myself the recipient of a grand reception, and a profusion of floral testimonials of regard from the ladies.

It was quite late before the last of my friends withdrew, and tired out, I was not long, I assure you, in seeking my pillow.

On glancing at the New York *World* the following morning, I read the following notice: "Daniel F. Beatty, Esq., of Washington, N. J., returned yesterday by the steamer City of Richmond. He has spent the entire summer in England, Germany, and France, placing agencies for the sale of his renowned Pianos and Organs. The demand for his instruments exceeds his anticipations."

The greater part of the day was spent in visiting my many business friends, and making preparations, after my brief respite, to engage once more in business pursuits.

A telegraph from Washington, N. J., was received:

"Congratulations of the office force. Come at five. MANAGER."

5 o'clock P. M. saw me in the parlor sleeping-car off for Washington, N. J. And as we glide swiftly over the rail of the D. L. & W. R. R., the country never seemed to wear so cheering and bright a prospect, while each familiar scene seemed doubly dear to me after my sojourn in distant lands, and safe return to my native shore.

At Hackettstown, 12 miles from Washington, the train comes to a stand, when a young man enters the car, and hands me the following telegram:

"Washington, N. J.
"Sept. 30th,
"HON. DANIEL F. BEATTY.

"Brace up, get your right hand glove off; crowd immense."
"W. L. and C. P. HUFF."

I must confess I got somewhat nervous, as the staff that accompanied me made no mention as to any reception.

However I braced myself up, peeled off my right hand glove, and settled myself down like a willing victim to the slaughter.

From Hacketstown to Washington, the train skipped along lively, and it was not long before I heard the engineer blow his whistle to signal the switchman at his post, as it is here the Morris & Essex Division of the road ends, and the road diverges from the track to Easton, and takes a curve to the northwest for Scranton, Binghamton and Oswego

As the train slowed up to the depot, what was my astonishment at beholding a vast concourse of people.

And my heart took up the joyful refrain of the Washington Brass Band, as it struck up

> "Home again, Home again,
> From a foreign shore."

The whole city apparently had emptied itself of its people, and such a concourse of friends and happy faces it has never been my good fortune to see.

The first to greet me was one of the little boys of our city, who knew me well, and had pressed forward amid the crowd, determined to be the first to grasp my hand; then came Mr. followed by all the employees and citizens of the city. My father was waiting for me in a barouche and four which entering, a procession was formed from the dopot to the office, where upon entering I found packed with another crowd, and best of all, the happy smiling faces of a bevy of little children. The Band of Hope dressed in white, and all drawn up in handsome style, whose happy cheerful voices rang out in songs of welcome. The parlors and offices were all brilliantly illuminated in honor of the occasion, the celebration of which is graphically described in the Washington, N. J. "*Review*," from the columns of which I clip the following:

"HOME AGAIN—A CORDIAL RECEPTION EXTENDED TO MR. DANIEL F. BEATTY UPON HIS RETURN FROM EUROPE.—On Sunday afternoon, September 29th, at 3 o'clock, the steamer City of Richmond, from Liverpool, arrived in the harbor of New York. Among her passengers was our townsman, Mr. Daniel F. Beatty, who, after a tour of several months through Europe, was on his way home. Mr. Beatty remained at one of the leading hotels in New York until Monday afternoon, when he left that city for homes arriving here at half-past seven o'clock. He wa, met at the railway station by a large number of our most prominent citizens, accompanied by the Washington Band. Immediately on his appearance on the platform, the band struck up a lively air, and the crowd pressed upon Mr. Beatty to take him by the hand. After a hand shake all around, the barouches in waiting were entered, and the procession, headed by the band, and an immense torchlight procession, moved down Washington Avenue to Beatty Building, which had been brilliantly illuminated in honor of the occasion.

"Previous to the starting of the procession from the railway station, the Band of Hope, numbering about one hundred and fifty young people, marched from the M. E. Church to Beatty Building, and with others, filled the spacious rooms on the second floor. Upon the arrival of the procession in front of the building, Mr. Beatty alighted from his carriage, and as he made his way, was greeted with the sweet strains of a 'Welcome,' played upon the piano by Prof. Lawrence, leader of the orchestra at the Delaware Water Gap House. On entering the parlor he was subjected to a rigorous hand-shaking, and welcomed home by an appropriate piece sang by the Band of Hope. Then Master Harry Dildine, son of Prof. W. M. Dildine, delivered the following address on behalf of the Band of Hope:

"'MR. BEATTY—RESPECTED SIR:—Permit me, on behalf of the Band of Hope, to welcome you once more to your native land, and to your own home. Among the many who have shown themselves liberal in benevolent and religious enterprises in our city, no name is more highly appreciated by the Band of Hope than that of Daniel F. Beatty. One of your Golden Tongue Organs, which you presented to us before leaving this continent, has contributed very much to make our meetings interesting. Having received the organ while the City of Chester, upon which you were a passenger, was crossing the great Atlantic, this is the first opportunity we have had to express to you our thanks. Allow me to say that you have a place in our memory—we have missed you. Again I say, on behalf of the Band of Hope, that we welcome your return to Washington.'

"The address was suitably responded to, and then Miss Sallie Spangenberg stepped forward and presented Mr. Beatty with a beautiful bouquet. The reception ceremonies being over, the members of the Band of Hope filed through the parlor, each one being taken by the hand by Mr. Beatty as they passed out.

"The reception lasted until a late hour, the guests making themselves at home in the handsomely furnished rooms devoted to the transaction of the Piano and Organ Business, for which the proprietor has established a world-wide reputation.

"Mr. Beatty has cause to feel proud of his

welcome home, for it was no doubt the largest demonstration ever made for a similar purpose in this town. And when it is considered that so little notice was given of the time and place of reception, it should be doubly gratifying to the recipient that so many of his friends were present to extent a welcome home."

The object of our mission would not be complete if we failed to present to our many readers the lessons these sights and scenes have taught, and from which we may draw a moral more forcible than any work that fiction could present.

Comparing the political institutions of America with continental Europe, we find ourselves more than ever attached to our own dear native land.

The "divine right of kings" is merely upheld and perpetuated by the power held by the hereditary few, around whose thrones the bristling bayonets of millions stand as slaves, ready, as "food for powder," to obey the mandate of kings, whose highest ambition consists in watching with jealous eyes the slightest encroachment of surrounding nations upon the boundary lines which divide them, every inch of which has been the scene of long contested strife, rich with the blood of myriads who have died upon the field of so called glory, not in the name of "Liberty," but to bind their posterity in stronger chains, and to enable the few to live in regal splendor upon the toil of the impoverished masses, whose aspirations dare not look beyond the sphere of their own limited circle.

Upon the monuments of imperial Europe are engraved imperishable lessons which the true statesman may well read and be admonished; to foster and develope the political institutions of our own native land, where the Godess of Liberty, enshrined in the hearts of her countrymen, points to the only true royalty, which springs from the will of the people, standing as the bulwark of the nation upon whose eternal foundations are written

TRUTH, JUSTICE AND LIBERTY.

And now dear reader, having accompanied me from the Blarney Stone of Old Ireland to Merrie England, from La Belle France to the sunny climes of Italy, and from the crater's mouth viewed the terror of Vesuvius, or the ancient ruins of Pompeii, thence down the picturesque Rhine, through Germany, and passing over the Alps of Switzerland gazed with me from the dizzy heights of hoary headed Mont Blanc, that like some grim sentry stands watch, century upon century, it is now time to remind my readers that, while hand in hand with me he has been enjoying, I trust, all the "sight seeing," I have on the other hand been busily engaged in projects calculated to extend my business to such an extent that the Beatty celebrated Piano and Organ shall be a household word as familiar amid the remote fastness of the Alps or the romantic highlands of Scotland as it is in our own dear native land.

Wherever my footsteps have wandered, whether in the crowded and fashionable salons of England, France or Germany, I found my name and the fame of my instruments had preceded me.

It was no strange occurrence to find my Pianos among the elite of France, the nobility of Germany, or the ivy clad towers of ancient England, and, need I say, inspired with this prestige and renown, together with the confidence that my justly celebrated instruments have inspired among even the crowned heads of Europe, I determined more than ever to push their sale to their utmost capacity. Already since my return have I began to feel the effects of my "Travels through Foreign Lands;" already am I in receipt of orders, which had it not been for the persistency with which I have pushed and introduced my instruments in continental Europe, some other enterprising foreign house might have reaped the benefit. My export trade has become extremely large.

And now dear reader I bid you adieu, should you at any time desire to see me or witness to your satisfaction the operations of my extensive business, remember that you are always cordially and at all times

"WELCOME".

to the parlors of the BEATTY BUILDING, and that every courtesy will be shown every one who contemplates a visit to the extensive Piano and Organ Establishment of DANIEL F. BEATTY, of Washington, New Jersey, United States of America.

THE END.

☞ THE BEATTY PIANO AND ORGAN MANUFACTORY,
Corner Rail Road Avenue and Beatty Street, Washington, New Jersey, United States of America.

The Beatty Piano and Organ Factory,

(From the N. Y. Scientific American.)

"The view represents Mr. Beatty's new factory, situated on Railroad Avenue, corner Beatty street, in the city of Washington, New Jersey. The small building in the foreground is the office belonging to the factory. The larger building is the new factory. The building seen some little distance behind the new factory is the Beatty Building, a spacious structure, containing in addition to the Beatty Music Hall proper, the office devoted to the extensive business connected with the piano and organ factory.

We have chosen a few only of the departments of this concern, as space will not permit us to enter into all of the details of piano and organ manufacture.

Everything in this factory is conducted on a perfect system. None but the best of workmen are employed, none but the best of materials are used, and the most modern machinery and appliances are adopted to facilitate the work and to render it not only cheaper but better.

Mr. Beatty's offices are extensive and well appointed. It requires twenty or more assistants to attend to the details of this immense business. The advertising bureau alone keeps a goodly number of persons constantly employed.

The business, started but a few years ago by its proprietor without a dollar, has grown beyond all precedent, amounting at present to several millions of dollars a year.

Mr. Beatty was lately elevated to the Mayoralty of Washington entirely without his own seeking. His fellow-citizens chose him. He conducted no campaign, and was not even present on election day, business having called him to New York on that day, and the news of his triumph was telegraphed to his headquarters at the Fifth Avenue Hotel. He bears his honors modestly, and his neighbors testify to his being the same genial, open-handed, free-hearted man as ever, not forgetting to relieve the unfortunate, to give freely to his church, nor deeming it beneath him to preside at Children's Day services in his own church.

The Beatty piano and organ are everywhere known. Mayor Beatty's success has been rapid and complete, and he claims to possess to-day the largest manufactory of pianos and organs which sells directly to the people."

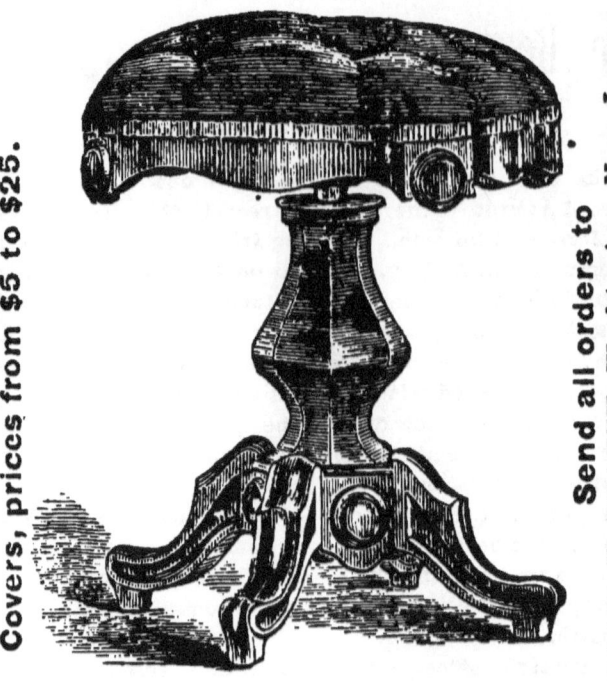

Beatty's Piano and Organ Stools, prices from $3 to $20, according to quality, also on hand, a large assortment of Covers, prices from $5 to $25.

Send all orders to DAN'L F. BEATTY. Washington, New Jersey.

ONLY 25 CENTS.

OVER SIXTY
Waltzes, Polkas, Marches, Galops, Operatic Melodies, Dances, Etc.

Beatty's Piano & Parlor Organ Instructor

Containing the elements of music with easy and progressive exercises to perfect the player in the art of music (either Piano or Organ) to which is added over Sixty Waltzes, Polkas, Marches, Galops, Operatic Melodies, Dances, etc., by Daniel F. Beatty; one of the best works of its kind ever introduced, and should be in the hands of every Piano and Organ player. Sent post paid to any part of the United States and Canada, for only Twenty-five Cents, the price having been reduced to introduce it everywhere.

Address,

DANIEL F. BEATTY, Washington, New Jersey.

PRICE TEN CENTS.

"BEATTY'S TOUR IN EUROPE"

IN

"FOREIGN LANDS"

OR

"EUROPE AS I SAW IT"

++ BY ++

DANIEL F. BEATTY,

Washington, New Jersey.

••

DANIEL F. BEATTY, Publisher,
Corner of Rail Road Avenue and Beatty Street,
Washington, New Jersey, United States of America.

1880.

"Beatty's Tour in Europe."

☞ To circulate this little book I will give special rates to News Agents and those who desire to get up a large club.

For full particulars,

Address,

DANIEL F. BEATTY,
Publisher,
Washington, New Jersey.

DANIEL F. BEATTY'S
CELEBRATED
PIANOS and ORGANS

Read what is said of them.

J. L. Everitt, Esq., Cashier National Broadway Bank, New York City, writes: "Organ received. As I am fully satisfied with the instrument, I remit without further delay. I have not thought it necessary to call in experts to test it. All my family are delighted with it."

G. H. Ware, Cashier Merchants' National Bank, Waterville, Maine, writes: "Piano proves satisfactory in every particular. I am no judge of musical instruments myself, but several *who are competent to judge* have tried it, and say the tone is very fine." *After a year's use.*—"With prices equal, I would as soon take my chances with him, and with prices decidedly in his favor, I would take his in preference should I wish to purchase again. We like the Piano very much."

H. H. Warner, Watertown, N. Y., writes: "Your Organ gives complete satisfaction. It cannot, in fact, be beat by any Organ of any make, containing the same number of reeds, for purity, sweetness and power of tone, or ease and rapidity of action. My daughters are highly delighted with it, and desire me to say that it is the best Organ they ever heard or saw, and that they would not part with it for half a dozen Monopolist Organs, which are sold at such an enormous price."

Wm. M. Daniells, South Alabama, N. Y., writes: "The Organ you shipped me I believe to be a better instrument for the money than ever was set up in Genesee County. Agents denounce your instruments, declaring them and you a humbug. The opposition, and dishonest and false statements I encounter in trying to introduce your instruments, is simply astonishing. I had no idea that men, claiming to be honest dealers, could stoop to anything so low."

Dr. E. B. Detchon, Crawfordsville, Ind., writes: It has been about nine months since we received our beautiful Piano from you, and must acknowledge, in all candor, that we are perfectly delighted with it. In fact, we regard our 'Beatty' instrument superior in beauty of style and appearance to almost any instrument in the city which cost twice or three times as much as ours. For richness of tone, beauty, power, volume and sweetness of expression, there are very few instruments that come up to the 'Beatty' Piano. Your instruments speak for themselves, and you will get more orders from this place."

☞ Send for long list from all parts of the World. ☜

Address,

DANIEL F. BEATTY,
Washington, New Jersey.

DANIEL F. BEATTY'S
CELEBRATED
PIANOS and ORGANS

GRAND, SQUARE AND Upright

PIANOS

Golden Tongue, Church, Hall, Chapel, Cabinet or Parlor

ORGANS

Upright Piano.

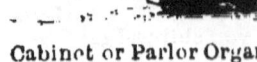

Cabinet or Parlor Organ.

NEW PIANOS, COVER, STOOL AND BOOK, Extremely **LOW For Cash**

Square Grand Piano.

NEW ORGANS, STOOL AND BOOK, $55 and Upwards

Before you purchase a Piano or Organ be sure send for my latest Circulars, &c.

Address, **DANIEL F. BEATTY**, Washington, New Jersey

www.ingramcontent.com/pod-product-compliance
Lightning Source LLC
Chambersburg PA
CBHW020147170426
43199CB00010B/926